SCENERY
AND
DIORAMAS

SCENERY

Chilton Book Company, Radnor, Pennsylvania

AND DIORAMAS

Robert Schleicher

Illustrations by
David Etchells

Copyright © 1983 by Robert Schleicher
All Rights Reserved
Published in Radnor, Pennsylvania 19089, by
Chilton Book Company
and simultaneously in Canada by
Fleet Publishers, a Division of
International Thomson Limited,
1410 Birchmount Road, Scarborough, Ontario M1P 2E7

Designed by William E. Lickfield
Manufactured in the United States of America

Library of Congress Cataloging in Publication Data
Schleicher, Robert H.
    Scenery and dioramas.
    Includes index.
    1. Models and modelmaking. 2. Diorama.
I. Title.
TT154.S3477   1983   745.592'8   82-45879
ISBN 0-8019-7221-3
ISBN 0-8019-7222-1 (pbk.)

1 2 3 4 5 6 7 8 9 0   2 1 0 9 8 7 6 5 4 3

To the members of the SLIM GAUGE GUILD HO SCALE MODEL RAILROAD CLUB, who proved that the real world—not some other modeler—provides the best inspiration for even a spectacular mountain scene. To the members of the SVERNA PARK MODEL RAILROAD CLUB, who proved that a city can be used as effective scenery. And, most particularly, to those modelers who realize that a diorama is truly a work of art. You have made it possible for me to show in these pages that scenery is a valuable expression of artistry, and that artistic scenery is easy to achieve.

Contents

List of Reference Cards

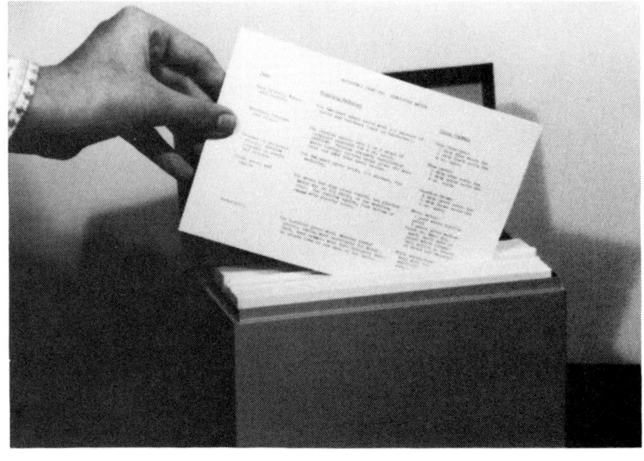

Make photocopies of the Reference Cards and this list, and place the set in a file box for instant reference. The text explains each scenery process in great detail; these procedures are condensed on the cards for ease of use.

"

Chapter 1

Scenery and Dioramas

The model builder is often considered more a technician than an artist. And this is true if you are simply snapping together a plastic-model car kit or running a toy train around a plugged-together track. But once you paint the model or add even a simple structure or two to a toy train, you are entering the realm of the artist. In fact, *anyone* who re-creates scenery in miniature is an artist. The simple act of duplicating or, in the case of some architectural models, *suggesting* scenery is as much of an art form as painting with pastels or oils. Creating a three-dimensional scene, such as a diorama or model railroad, combines the artistic skills of the sculptor and the painter. The ultimate development of the modeler-as-artist, of course, is embodied in the dioramas in museums, particularly in science and industry museums. These scenes were created by professional modelers, but you do not have to be a professional to create a scene of artistic value.

The techniques used to re-create nature and its effects in three-dimensional miniatures have been so refined and simplified over the years that anyone with the skill to snap together a plastic kit can create a realistic scene. If you apply the lessons in this book to any scene, you will have produced a work of art.

Architectural and Topographic Models

Most of the techniques in this book go one step beyond building architectural models, since the purpose of most architectural models is to provide a conceptual image of the terrain and landscaping that will complement a proposed structure. It is easier to envision the

Fig. 1–1 The effect of the Slim Gauge Guild's HO-scale scenery is spectacular, but its methods are so simple that anyone can follow them.

entire scene from these models than from a plan or isometric drawing. But even the model is often a relatively simple version of the final scene. The subtle effects of shading and weathering that are added to a military diorama or model railroad scene are not needed on architectural models.

The architectural model can take several forms, ranging from a rough outline of the structure itself to a complete scene that includes

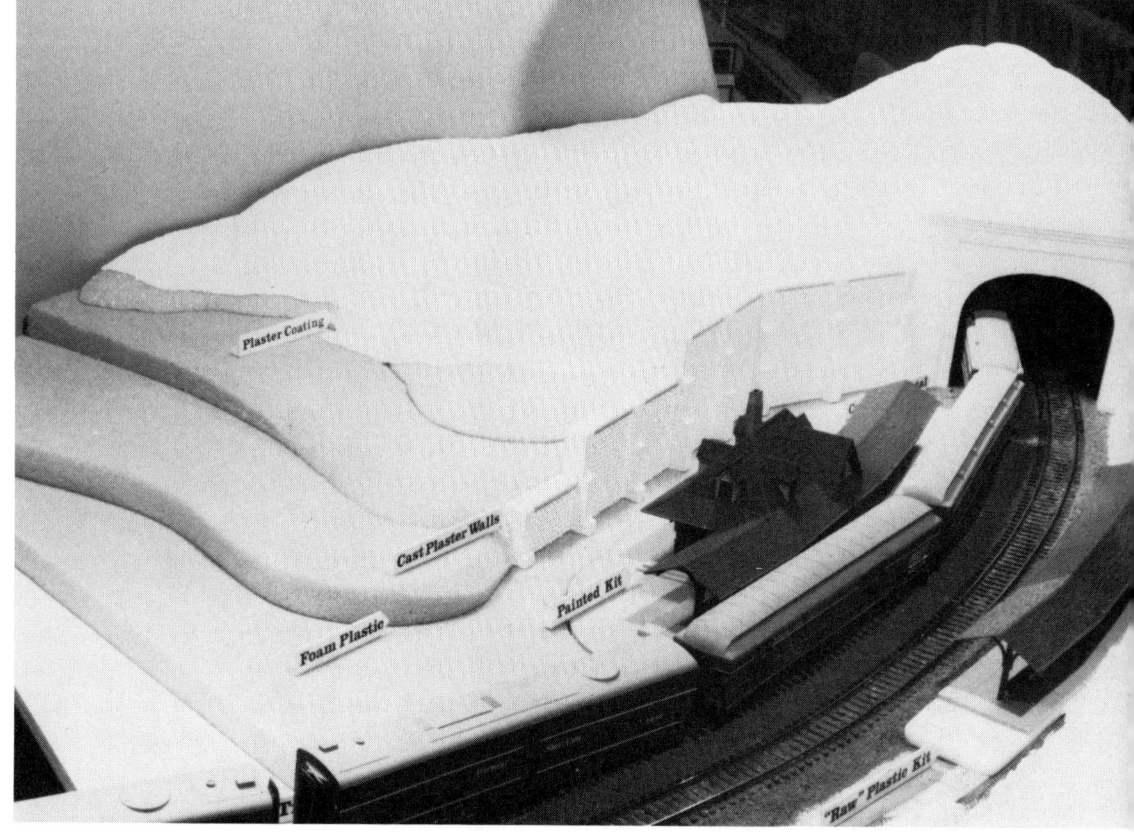

Fig. 1–2 For featherweight scenery, shape contour profiles in polyfoam insulating board, as was done in this scene made by the Pittsburgh HO-Scale Modular Club.

the structure, the surrounding terrain, trees and shrubs, and often people and vehicles. When the architectural model includes the surrounding terrain as well as the structure, it is called a topographic model. The topographic designation applies when the scope of the model includes more terrain than structure—for example, a complete housing or industrial development, where structures occupy only a fraction of the available acreage.

The amount of detail on a landscaping model and, in fact, its actual scale can vary considerably. Some landscaping models for housing or industrial developments are built to a scale as small as 1/100 to show the number and position of trees, streets, sidewalks, and grassy areas.

Other landscaping models might be built to a scale as large as the 1/24-scale model in Figure 1–3. The most common architectural modeling scales are shown in Figure 1–4.

Dioramas

The creation of a model aircraft, military tank, or model railroad locomotive used to be a complete project in itself. We could use our

Fig. *1–3* AMSI's professional modelers created this $\frac{1}{24}$-scale landscaping model using the firm's ground foam, fiber, and tree trunk kits.

Fig. 1–4 MODEL-SCALE PROPORTIONS

Scale	Other Designations for the Same Scale	Common Uses
1/220	Z	trains
1/160	N	trains
1/100	—	architectural models
1/87	HO	trains
1/80	—	architectural models
1/76	British: 00 scale (4mm = 1′)	military models and trains
1/72	1″ = 6′	military and ship models
1/64	S $\frac{3}{16}$″ = 1′	architectural models and trains
1/60	—	architectural models
1/50	—	architectural models
1/48	O $\frac{1}{4}$″ = 1′	trains, aircraft and military models
1/40	—	architectural models
1/35	—	military models
1/32	$\frac{3}{8}$″ = 1′	architectural models, aircraft, car, and ship models
1/25	—	model cars
1/24	$\frac{1}{2}$″ = 1′	architectural models, model cars, and dollhouses
1/16	$\frac{3}{4}$″ = 1′	architectural models
1/12	1″ = 1′	dollhouses and architectural models
1/10	—	architectural models
1/8	$1\frac{1}{2}$″ = 1′	architectural models
1/1	full-scale 12″ = 1′	movie, TV, and theater sets and props

imaginations to envision how the model appeared in real life. Today, most modelers go beyond the model itself and create a *diorama*—the model as well as its environment or historical context. Since nearly every model is part of a historical scene (or, in some cases, a scene from the future or from a fantasy world), the techniques developed by professional model makers to create those scenes are precisely the ones the amateur modeler should follow. Weathering a model airplane so that it looks just as it does in flight is one form of diorama. However, if you are modeling a military tank, a race car, a steam locomotive, or a Victorian house, the model will almost always have a "missing" part; the "scenery" supplies that missing part. Some modelers even feel that a model military tank, race car, or Victorian house is just a toy until it is placed in its natural setting.

For most modelers, the constraints of time and space demand that only a few models be placed in dioramas. The model railroader can complete not only a railroad station but also the station platform, parking lot, and other surrounding details. This station diorama can exist on its own on a bookshelf until the model railroad itself is ready for the station "scene." Then the station as well as the surroundings can be arranged and set in place.

Scenery Made Simple: The Reference Cards

The "scenery made simple" techniques here are designed to allow anyone to complete an artistically perfect scene, including subtle texture and shading effects, in as little time as possible. You will find twenty-five Reference Cards that provide virtually all the information you need to create any scene in this book. For easy reference, photocopy the pages on 5 × 8 cards on a Xerox machine or other dry copier and file them in a file-card case or recipe box. Protect the cards by spraying them with several thick coats of Testors "Dullcote" or a similar flat-finish clear paint. Then they will be handy when you truly are in the hands-on phase of building scenery. The formulas on the Reference Cards use water-soluble materials wherever possible, so you can proceed through the entire process in just a single evening without having to wait for one step to "dry." The materials noted contain the lowest amount of toxic substances and have the least odor.

Some of the suggestions, such as the extensive use of ground foam for texture and artist's matte medium for cement, rather than dyed sawdust for texture and white glue, are more costly than their alternatives. In every instance, however, the lower-cost alternative is *not* as realistic, or it has some other fault: For example, white glue can crack, whereas matte medium is flexible. Near-equal choices of materials will be noted, such as deciding whether to search for a realistic

Nine-Step Scenery the Simple Way

Step	Procedure	Chapter
1.	Locate photographs and color samples of real-life scenes	1 and 2
2.	Build basic shape in Celluclay or plaster	1, 2, 3, and 4
3.	Add any rock castings or cliffs	2 and 4
4.	Color surfaces with water-base paints	1 and 4
5.	Apply sifted dirt, ground foam, or other texture	3, 4, 5, 8, and 11
6.	Install trees and bushes	6
7.	Install ponds, streams, rivers, and other water effects	7
8.	Install structures, people, and other man-made features	1, 3, and 8
9.	Apply weathering with water-base paints	1, 4, 8, and 10

tree trunk rather than purchasing Woodland Scenics' or AMSI's cast-metal trunks. In these examples, the commercial product noted produces results equal to "natural" growth, and they also can save countless hours of searching. *Don't* be intimidated by the "Do's and Don't's" (Reference Card 2). *Do* follow the charts. Only examples of the "do" techniques have been selected for this book. *Don't* examples can be found in nearly every issue of hobby magazines. There are exceptions to these rules. If you are an accomplished artist, you may be able to paint a backdrop that is as effective as those sold by HO West! or Detail Associates, or the photomurals from Vollmer or Faller. You may even have developed a technique to "tease" sawdust so that it looks like grass. The purpose of the "don't" charts is to point out some techniques you may have read about but haven't tried—techniques that are too smelly, toxic, time-consuming, or unrealistic, or a combination of any of these undesirable qualities. This book offers you the experiences of more than a dozen professional architectural modelers and diorama builders and skilled amateurs, as well as *effective* commercial products. These methods are not only the most realistic, but they are nearly failureproof because they have been proven by use.

Building a Basic Diorama

The best way to learn any new skill is to dive right in with both hands. You can build a simple 1 × 1 foot-square diorama on a single ceiling tile or scrap of plywood for little cost and learn much about scenery building in the process. The diorama can be even smaller than a foot square if you simply want to create a small scene for 54mm (approximately 1/32 scale) military miniatures. The larger diorama will be adequate for displaying a piece of armor (Fig. 1–5), a barge-loading coaling trestle (Figs. 1–6 and 1–7), or a racing-garage scene (Fig. 1–8). The completed diorama can be glued to the back of a custom-made picture frame (see Fig. 1–5) for display on a bookshelf, or it can be included eventually in a complete model railroad.

Keep your first diorama as simple as possible. For the diorama in Figure 1–5, George DeWolfe used a flat piece of plywood covered with Celluclay, artist's matte medium, and gravel for the basic scenery. His Sherman tank (a 1/32-scale Monogram kit) and Russian peasant hut (with a Testors/Italeri Panzer IV tank) are featured in the color

The Basic Do's and Don'ts for Realistic Scenery

1. DO arrange lighting so that the background receives slightly more light than the foreground.
    DON'T build or color scenery under any lighting other than that used on the layout or diorama.

2. DO precolor *all* plaster or hydrocal so that no white shows.
    DON'T try to paint every nook and cranny in the plaster.

3. DO apply a color wash to match the predominant earth color on all buildings and ground cover.
    DON'T place contrasting earth colors (such as red and beige) next to each other.

4. DO spray on a wash of light olive green to trees and shrubs to blend their colors.
    DON'T use out-of-the-box lichen moss or other texture that is Kelly green without treating and coloring it.

5. DO use coal, petrified wood, and real rocks as patterns for latex rubber molds.
    DON'T use real rocks as is for scenery.

6. DO use 1:1 epoxies or artist's gloss medium to simulate water.
    DON'T use casting resin and catalyst or real water to simulate water.

7. DO use rock castings or retaining walls for slopes steeper than 45 degrees.
    DON'T apply grass or weeds to slopes steeper than 45 degrees.

(continued)

The Basic Do's and Don't's for Realistic Scenery, *continued*

8. DO include some gentle dirt- and weed-covered slopes beside tracks.
   DON'T use *only* rock cliffs or retaining walls on slopes beside tracks.

9. DO measure and record everything used in mixing plaster, colors, and resins so that you can duplicate them.
   DON'T attempt to match a color just by dabbing on a similar color.

10. DO refer to color pictures in magazines as prototypes for *all* scenery shapes and colors.
   DON'T try to duplicate someone else's scenery.

11. DO install a wraparound sky blue backdrop (shaded to gray-blue at the horizon).
   DON'T paint anything other than sky and clouds on a backdrop.

12. DO build mountains or background city buildings at eye level.
   DON'T place any backdrop where the horizon is below eye level.

13. DO use several shades and sizes of ground foam, real dirt, and flocking for all "loose" textures.
   DON'T use untreated lichen, colored sawdust, or real pebbles for scenery.

14. DO use the exact "natural" shades shown in the color charts for *all* colors.
   DON'T use "solid" colors such as black, white, green, yellow, or brown for any scenery effects.

Fig. 1–5 A painted and weathered Testors/Italeri $\frac{1}{35}$-scale Panzer I tank is the focal point of George De-Wolfe's military diorama.

Fig. 1–6 This turn-of-the-century coaling dock won a prize for Irv Schultz in the NMRA national contest.

Fig. 1–7 The coaling dock diorama later became an integral part of Irv Schultz's HO-scale model railroad.

section. The basic diorama for these two scenes is only a slightly higher pile of Celluclay with a greater variety in rock and rubble size.

Planning the Scene

The artistic effect in George DeWolfe's prize-winning dioramas is no accident. George has been a professional artist and photographer, and photography in particular showed him the importance of balance and composition. George follows six simple rules to ensure that his dioramas are realistic re-creations:

1. Each diorama is like a frame from a cartoon or a TV storyboard. It implies action and captures a fleeting moment.
2. There is enough "world" around each figure or vehicle to imply that the world continues beyond the scene.
3. None of the elements of the diorama, not even the cobblestone road, is parallel to the edge or frame of the scene.
4. The major point of emphasis in each scene is shifted slightly away from the center to give balance to the rest of the scene.
5. Each diorama is composed so that the viewer's eye is led from one element to the next. This allows the entire scene to be appreciated.
6. The weathering on the figures and vehicles is blended into the ground colors so that the entire scene becomes a world in itself.

Building from the Ground Up

The dioramas in this chapter incorporate techniques from nearly every other chapter. Start the simplest diorama by mixing about a half-cup of Celluclay (or Gold Seal's "Modern Mâché") with water as indicated on the side of the package. Because Celluclay and "Modern Mâché" papier-mâché products contain extra binders and cements, they are much better than the traditional newspaper-and-wallpaper-paste papier-mâché formula. They can be spread as thin as $\frac{1}{16}$ inch over as much as a 12 × 12-inch-square surface without cracking. However, the surface must be supported on a picture frame or base so that it will not flex and cause the Celluclay to crack. The Celluclay can also be built up to be an inch or so thick for small hills or lumps in a roadway. For elevations of more than $\frac{1}{4}$ inch, wadded-up wet newspapers are best.

If you are going to run a railroad track across the diorama, use the

Fig. 1–8 Parts from a half-dozen $\frac{1}{25}$-scale plastic car kits and some strips and sheets of balsa wood were used for Tom Reed's diorama.

cork roadbed to elevate the track and to simulate the ballast shoulders. (If you are building it at an oblique angle, remember Rule 3.) The cork roadbed can be used to simulate elevated highways, with several strips placed parallel to one another. Don't cover the cork with Celluclay for a railroad right-of-way, but do cover it to simulate dirt or paved roads. You'll find all the information that you need on roads and roadbeds in Chapter 3.

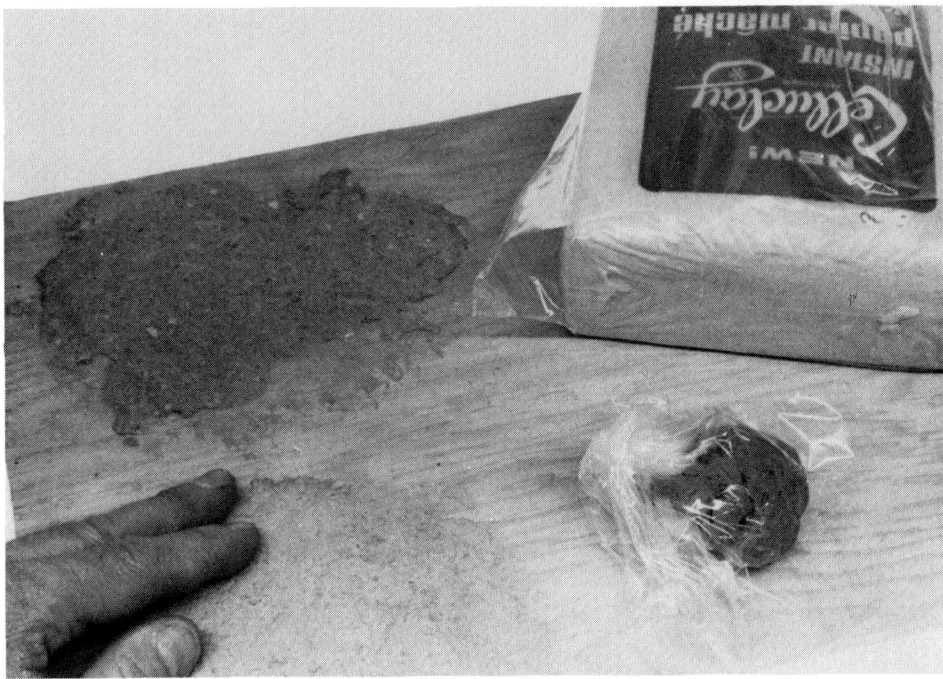

Fig. 1–9 Celluclay can be spread into a thin layer to provide texture and uneven ground shapes.

If you are going to use any large rocks or other details, such as a piece of bombed-out wall, push them into the Celluclay while it is still wet. When the Celluclay dries, it will approximate rough scale-model earth. You can color it with Polly S earth colors (see Chapter 5) and sprinkle on some loose, sifted dirt before adding vehicles and figures. If you cannot locate Celluclay, substitute "Modern Mâché."

A basic earth-colored Celluclay diorama can be the starting point for an endless array of fine details. Several layers of sifted dirt held in place with water and artist's matte medium can produce a rutted road. Before you add the vehicles and figures, read every chapter and pick one element from each to include on this "practice" diorama. You can add rock castings, weeds, trees, puddles of water, and even ice and snow. The close-up detailing possibilities are endless. You could even add empty cans and other debris. This diorama is also the place to practice weathering and people-painting techniques. If you make a mess, scrape off what you can, cover it with another layer of Celluclay, and start over.

A Piece of the Whole

Irv Schultz is a master at creating dioramas that later become part of his permanent model railroad layout. The barge-loading coal dock in Figure 1–6 is shown as it was when entered in the diorama division of a National Model Railroad Association contest. Figure 7 shows it nestled into Irv's model railroad. Complete model railroad scenes can be planned into your existing railroad, or you can plan some future railroad to include several scenes you have built over the years and had no space for.

Don't let the diorama format discourage you from using several track elevations and other multilevel scenes. It is relatively easy to plan a model railroad to fit minor differences in the elevations of sidings. Be sure to keep an accurate record of all color and texture formulas you use so that you can match old scenery to new.

Modular Model Railroads:
The Ultimate Diorama

The practical limit on the size of a single diorama is about 24 × 24 inches. Anything larger is usually too heavy for a bookcase or shelf. If you have 24 × 48 inches of available space, however, why not consider making a portion of a complete model railroad—a module. A module is either a section of a larger model railroad or just large enough to incorporate as many as a half-dozen individual diorama scenes. The modular model railroading concept is simple: You build a 2 × 4-foot section of the railroad with the extreme ends matched to the extreme ends of hundreds of other 2 × 4-foot sections. Because of the interfacing ends, any one module can be connected to another to create a model railroad two feet wide and as long as there are modules. It is also possible to construct a few buildings on 6 × 6- or 6 × 12-inch boards and incorporate them into a module.

Several N-, HO-, and O-scale modular standards exist, and there are literally thousands of modules. Most major cities have a modular model railroad club that meets about once a month to assemble a layout with the members' modules. David Smith's HO-scale desert scene (Fig. 1–10) is an example of one module that was connected to

Fig. 1–10 David Smith used bent pipe cleaners, MLR cactus, lichen, and ground foam to simulate the sparse Arizona desert vegetation in HO scale.

others'. The club supplies the 4 × 4-foot corner modules, so the resulting layout is O-shaped with space for the operators inside the "O" and spectator areas around the outside. More information, with actual benchwork patterns and dozens of track plans for N- and HO-scale modular layouts also can be found in Volume 3 of *The Model Railroading Handbook*.

Modules and dioramas have one feature in common: They provide enough space in a *small* space for some real model railroading—from buildings to scenery to train switching operations.

Chapter 2

Imitating Nature

One of the major mistakes that modelers make is to try to duplicate someone else's model, rather than nature. Although it may seem easier to match the scenery of another modeler, the opposite is true: The *best* you can hope for is a caricature of the model. This book offers you all the techniques you need to duplicate the scenery of the professional diorama builders and gifted amateurs. What you will not find here, of course, is nature itself. For that, you must go directly to the source.

The research involved in finding the scene for your diorama can be fun in itself, and it will increase your appreciation of the world around you at the same time. The best way to begin is to combine vacations and weekend trips with your hobby. A second way is to search for color photographs of the scene you have in mind. Before you set out on your quest, you should have some idea of the scene you want to duplicate. For example, if you are modeling the Rio Grande narrow gauge in Colorado's Rocky Mountains, try to plan a vacation there. A trip to the Sierra Nevadas won't help. This is another reason why it's a mistake to copy a model: You have no way of knowing whether the modeler actually researched the scenery. If you cannot visit the area you want to model, try to find calendars, back issues of magazines like *National Geographic,* or large illustrated books such as those series published by Time-Life or the "on sale" illustrated books in large bookstores.

The paints, dyes, textures, and shapes are included here, but for their specific applications, you must do some research. Before you go into the real world, arm yourself with the *model* half of your project.

Fig. 2–1 Lee Nicholas created the floor-to-ceiling scenery on his HO-scale railroad from photographs.

Buy Floquil's Polly S color charts and Glidden color charts (Reference Card 7), or those of other paint brands, so that you can match the colors of nature. Buy a complete assortment of ground polyurethane foam greens and yellows too, and take everything with you on your field trip. Also take a camera and a notebook to record where you took each picture and which paint and ground foam colors most closely match the scene. You will have to take some artistic license here, of course. The colors in nature may be more intense or more faded than the color chip and ground foam samples. But you can correct for that when you paint the model, or you can alter the amount of light that falls on it.

Natural Lighting and Color Matching

To match colors to nature, match the color chips and ground foam textures to your color photographs. To bring the *effect* of nature's lighting indoors to your miniature scenery, you will have to make major color corrections. You will discover, for instance, that the color chips and ground foam samples do not match the colors in your photographs. Remember that you matched the color samples outside, as they appeared in sunlight, and that the developing process alters the color values of photos to some extent. Your color prints and pictures in books and magazines will help you determine what color the "dirt" really should be on your indoor scenery. And the notations you make when you match the color chips and ground foam to nature will help because most will likely be only a shade or two away from the closest match.

Do not try to match an actual rock or leaf to the color chips. Close-up color is seldom the same as the color of the entire tree or the color of rocks on a cliff. The color effect you need for a model is that seen from a greater distance. Fortunately, the reduced size of the scene in photographs is similar to the scale of your model. The highlights and shadows that will result from rock casting, earth texture, and ground foam will also provide the variations in shadow and highlight.

The Shape of Nature

Your research into the nature of nature will help you duplicate the illusive shape of the hillsides and foliage in the real world. The photographs will tell you two important things: what the major shape of the hillsides and trees should be, and how "rough" the shapes should be. For example, are the hills steep like the peaks of the Rocky Mountains, or are they gentle like the "hills" of Kansas? (A 45-degree slope is "steep" in nature.) Are the surfaces of the slopes rough like the exposed rock faces of the Rocky Mountains, or are they smooth like the grass-covered hills of Kentucky's Blue Grass area? The plaster or foam-plastic scenery will have to be shaped to match the degree of the slopes on your model. The rough texture of the hills can be duplicated with one of a variety of patterns for latex rubber "rock" molds (see Chapter 4).

Before you try to duplicate tree shapes, you will want to know whether to buy or build a trunk structure that will re-create, for example, the columnar shape of a cypress tree or the mushroom shape of an oak. The tree's texture can be smooth and carefully pruned or rough like an ancient pine. Both textures, and everything in between, can be duplicated with ground foam (see Chapter 6), but you must know the "natural" effect in order to duplicate it. Similar research will provide the data you need for weeds, roads, water, and all the other details that make the Rockies so much different from Kentucky's rolling hills.

Planning in Three Dimensions

One of the most common uses for scenery is to make a tabletop model railroad more realistic. Unfortunately, too many model railroaders confuse the *sequence* of railroad versus scenery. It is difficult to create credible scenery as an afterthought to the model railroad. The construction of the scenery should begin at the same time as the construction of the railroad—at the planning stage. For example, if you lay the track before you plan your embankment for a trestle, you will have to do a lot of bracing and build a lot of benchwork to provide a place for the embankment. So your mountains and valleys, cuts and fills, and tunnels and trestles should all be planned with at least as much precision as in laying the track. Hills and valleys, though, are more three-dimensional than track. If your mind does not translate two dimensions into three with ease, and few do, follow the lead of the most experienced model railroaders and build a model of your model.

Dr. Joseph Nicholls is one of those "most experienced" model railroaders. The National Model Railroad Association has awarded him a well-earned "Master Model Railroader" certificate of achievement. Dr. Nicholls knew that he had designed a complex model railroad, and he wanted to be certain that the tracks were separated enough to allow for a 45-degree or less slope along embankments between lower- and upper-level tracks. He drew a track plan of $1\frac{1}{2}$ inches to the foot (where $\frac{1}{8}$ inch equals 1 inch) so that he could duplicate structures with blocks of painted balsa. This model is a topographic or architectural model like those described in Chapter 1. Dr. Nicholls went so far as to cut small chunks of fine-pore sponge to represent the trees. His model took more time than many of us spend on our actual railroads, but it accomplished the goal more quickly than trying to adjust the track locations and scenery contours on the full-size HO-scale layout. He discovered, just from the section of the model shown in Figure 2–2, that the embankment in the upper left of the photo-

Fig. 2–2 Dr. Joseph Nichols made this $\frac{1}{16}$ inch: 1-foot model of his proposed HO-scale layout to ensure successful scenery.

graph was too steep: He solved the problem by reducing the uphill grade to lower the upper-level track.

Models and Mock-Ups

Sometimes you might want to make full-scale mock-ups of your proposed buildings or scenic features. The hill-building techniques in Chapter 4 allow you to shape *all* the basic contours with wadded-up, wet newspapers. Similar see-how-it-looks-before-you-build techniques can be used for model structures.

Robert Schlachter, who specializes in narrow-gauge prototypes, is one of the most skillful modelers in the United States. One of his latest projects is a modular model railroad depicting a two-foot narrow-gauge railroad of his own creation, but it is based on the Maine railroads of the 1920s. The shelf-style railroad leaves little room, particularly in O (1/4) scale, for the relatively large structures of a Maine seaside town. To be sure that his buildings would fit, he assembled cardboard mock-ups as shown in Figure 2–3. The passenger station, with its hexagonal bay and peaked roof, and the group of houses were modified several times to achieve the desired effect. Now the thin cardboard mock-ups can be used as patterns for the sheet styrene or basswood walls of the actual models. The same technique could of course be used to modify kit-built structures by making full-size duplicates on a photocopy machine or by tracing the wall outlines with a pencil onto cardboard. The kits then could be cut down to provide a balanced grouping.

Fig. 2–3 The shapes to the left of this 0-scale scene will later become buildings on Robert Schlachter's layout.

Geology for Modelers

Some experienced model railroaders claim that you need a college course in geology in order to create a realistic model. Nonsense. Instead, you need to develop the eye of the landscape artist and learn to observe the real world. For example: One of the better scenery builders discovered that the shape of broken coal was more like the shape of scale-model rock than most real rock. Like many modelers, he uses latex rubber to make flexible molds of broken coal for pre-colored plaster rock castings (see Chapter 4). This is the same type of skill that led modelers to discover that sagebrush twigs were almost exact scale-model tree trunks (see Chapter 6). For the modeler, actual observation of the lay of the land is more important than a geology course.

Of course, you should have a basic understanding of how nature operates so that you can avoid the most glaring mistakes in re-creating scenery in miniature. Mountains were formed as the earth's plates shifted and folded. Aside from earthquakes and a few active volcanoes, most of the earth's surface has been shaped by glaciers and by the erosion of wind and water. To the modeler, nature offers relatively few cliffs: Most of the mountains and hills look like those in Figure 2–4 on at least three of their sides. The cliffs in most areas appear only on one side of the hill or mountain where the land has faulted. The exceptions are the buttes associated with the southwestern desert and canyons formed by rivers.

Too many modelers concentrate on the cliff faces and ignore the more common gentle faces of hills and mountains. This is because they try to duplicate the efforts of other modelers, or because they did not plan their scene from the beginning and now lack adequate space.

The views in Figure 2–5 are the four most common hillside cuts. These cuts may eventually become tunnels if the walls become too high. There is no simple rule for determining whether a cut is deep enough, with the hilltop high enough above the tracks, to justify a tunnel. If the banks leading to the tunnel are steep, you will need less "mountain" over the tunnel. If the track cuts through earthen banks with slopes of about 30 to 45 degrees, the cut must be very deep indeed before a tunnel is necessary. Only exposed rock slopes are steeper than 45 degrees. A tunnel through such soft substance as dirt, loose rock, or sandstone is always lined with wood or stones (Fig. 2–6). The cut-

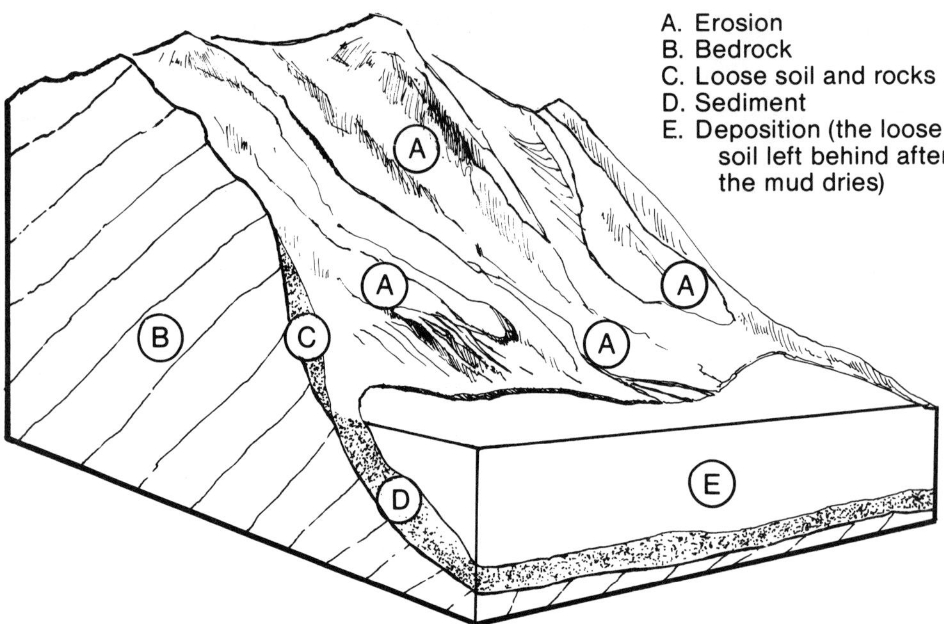

Fig. 2–4 A cutaway view of rock and dirt erosion from mountaintops and slopes.

aways in Figure 2–5 reveal some of the essential elements that are missing from many model railroads. The two most important features of any railroad cut are the drainage ditches on either side of the track.

Tunnels

The two tunnels in Figure 2–6 show how the relatively shallow tunnels so common on model railroads can be made more realistic. There is little cover over either of these tunnels because both go through rock rather than dirt. The important element here is that most of the mountain is *implied* as sloping up and away from the tunnel. If you must have short and shallow tunnels, make sure to include more of the mountain. The wall can be located to the left or the right of either tunnel in Figure 2–6. The edge of the table also can be located far to the right or left. Model railroaders tend to slope all mountains upward from the edge of the table, but you can achieve more realism by allowing some to slope up toward the aisle. Make sure, though, that any slopes between the tracks and the backdrop (except for the earthen fills or embankments made by the railroad) slope upward toward the

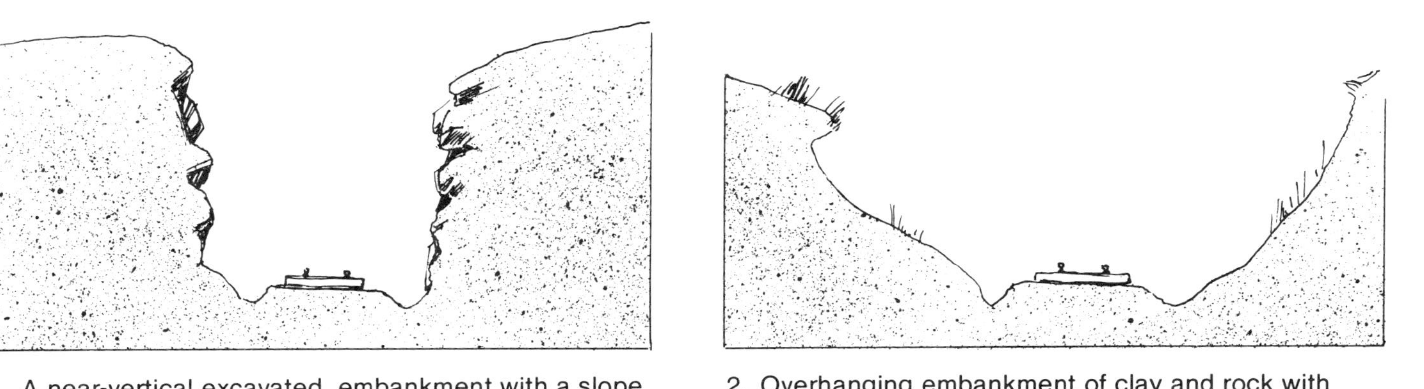

1. A near-vertical excavated embankment with a slope of 45° to 90°.

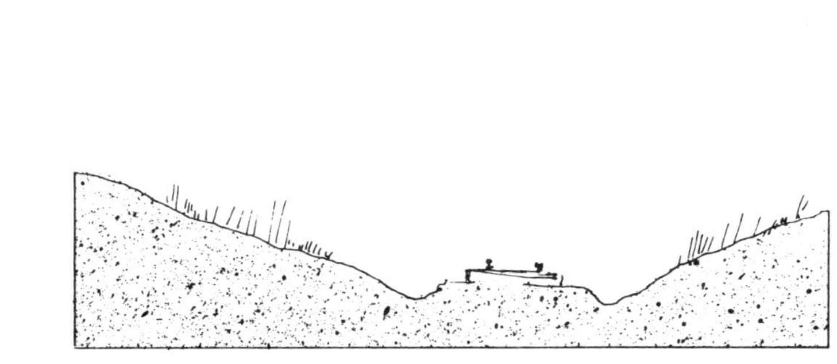

2. Overhanging embankment of clay and rock with slopes of 30° to 45°.

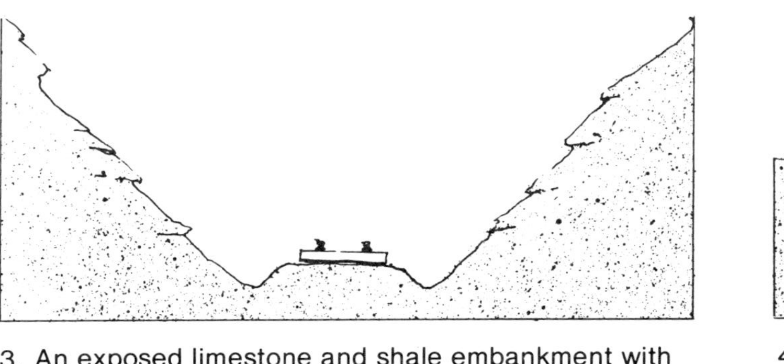

3. An exposed limestone and shale embankment with a 30° to 45° slope, usually covered with loose dirt and rocks.

4. The most common embankment, with slopes of 0° to 30°, usually covered with weeds.

Fig. 2–5 Four cutaway views of the type of terrain that creates different degrees of slopes in fills or cuts on either side of the track and drainage ditches.

Typical granite cliffs. Tunnel may have no linings or portals.

On limestone, sandstone, or shale cliffs, tunnels require wood, stone, or concrete linings and portals.

Fig. 2–6 Modelers often place tunnels through the center of mountains. Instead, place tunnels through the shoulders of rock cliffs.

backdrop. This will give the viewer's eye a natural path to follow toward the horizon.

Simulated Rocks

A background in geology is no more important to the model railroader than a background in chemistry is important to the amateur chef. And in the case of model scenery, knowing too much can actually be a disadvantage. For example, the actual color of any rock is *not* what you want to capture: What you want to re-create in miniature is the entire *effect* of a rocky cliff or the whole meadow or a complete tree. Matching color samples to actual leaves or blades of grass or rocks produces a toylike effect. If you expect your scenery to look real, you must try to duplicate a particular geographic area. The name of the rock, whether sandstone or granite, is not important. What you want to know about the rock is its color and texture and, beyond that, the shape of the hills on the tops and sides of the rocky cliffs.

Prepare a list to guide you in your search for natural materials. And take some color photographs along the way. Look for real rocks, pieces of broken coal, and even well-weathered driftwood that duplicate the texture (not necessarily the overall shape) of the rocky cliffs and cuts you want to model. Also look for weeds to use as trees or bushes and dirt to use as real dirt. The slopes and crests of hills can be formed with wadded-up newspapers to match the angles and shapes in your photographs. Start your list of natural items now, but read the other chapters for many of the other natural items you will need for a realistic diorama. Figure 4–6 shows four items that duplicate the surfaces of real rocks in exact scale. The lesson here is that textures suitable for model rocks do not necessarily come from *actual* rocks. If you cannot locate the type of rocks you need for your cliff faces, go to a rock or gem shop (these shops also have petrified wood) or look at different types of hard and soft coal.

In Chapter 4 you will find out how to use rocks or coal as patterns for latex rubber molds, which in turn will be used to make precolored plaster castings of the rocks. It also will show how to obtain the textural realism of real rocks or real coal. Never use real rocks to simulate rocks. They're far too heavy, their textures are out of scale for any model, and the colors are not realistic. The realism of a real rock is almost always destroyed when it is placed next to a scale-model human or animal figure.

Fig. 2–7 Master patterns of real rocks for latex rubber molds: (left to right) granite, petrified wood, coal, and (in foreground) lava.

Access Hatches for Model Railroads

Modern planning techniques for model railroads require benchwork that runs around the walls, with an occasional "peninsula" jutting into any available space in the center of the room. This system allows the operators and spectators to get closer to the trains. The benchwork is relatively narrow so that the modeler can reach the backdrop, and it allows the layout to be placed much higher than the older island-style layouts so that the horizon is closer to eye level, as described in Chapter 9. The higher the layout is placed, however, the narrower the shelf or peninsula must be; most of us can reach only about two feet without bending at the waist. One of the reasons for a conventional table-height model railroad was to provide for access; most of us can reach more than three feet if we can bend at the waist. The most realistic way to display your models is to elevate them to at least chest level, about 48 to 54 inches from the floor.

For some track plans, the only way to maintain that 24-inch maximum reach and keep the models high enough for proper viewing (and to allow for an eye-level horizon) is to provide a few access hatches in the center of the layout. Access hatches can be disguised with the edges of cliffs, or they can be placed behind the crests of mountains. The same scenic profile that hides the access hole usually hides the tracks behind it. The types of access holes that need the special scenic treatments in this chapter are those used strictly for emergency track repairs or for rerailing trains.

Planning for Access

It is not fun to have to crawl under a model railroad to reach an access hatch. And the task becomes formidable when you cannot even squeeze your shoulders through the hole. Access holes must be a minimum of 18 × 24 inches for most of us, and perhaps wider if you are broad shouldered. To be able to turn your body comfortably, 24 × 24 inches is even better. You will disguise the access hole in any case, so the extra few inches usually won't make much difference. Obviously, you don't want to place an access hole where a track can cross it; if your layout lacks even an 18 × 24-inch space, you have crammed in too many tracks.

The principle of a lift-out access hole is the same as the lift-out access panels into most attics; a support frame is built around the *underside* of the access hole and a piece of plywood is dropped in from the top. To open the hole, you simply push up tbe plywood and move it aside. The construction of the access hole, then, requires a frame of 1 × 2 boards around the underside of the hole, so when you plan for a 24 × 24-inch opening, make the actual opening a few inches larger. If you're crammed for every inch, simply butt the 1 × 2 support frame in the four corners, extending it out about 4 inches into the 24-inch

Fig. 2–8 The 24 × 24-inch access hole in Willard Jones's HO-scale railroad allows him to reach derailed locomotives easily.

sides. Even a simple diagonal support across each corner is fine. You won't touch the inside corners of the access hole when you move in or out of it, so the cut-off corners should not be a problem.

Camouflaging the Access Hatch

After you have completed the benchwork for your layout and the surrounding frame, supporting frame, and plywood cover for the access hatch (some layouts require more than one access area), pay particular attention to how the surrounding scenery will meet the edges of the hatch. The obvious solution is to camouflage the access

Fig. 2–9 A lake covers Willard Jones's 24 × 24-inch access hole. The straight edges are disguised by fallen trees, a road, dam, and coarse-ground foam.

hatch with a lake, which is what Willard Jones did in Figures 2–8 and 2–9. It is also possible to make only the "water" portion of the lake removable. You will have to hinge the corner braces so that you can drop the access hole (and the lake) downward to remove it. With this technique, use a coping saw or a saber saw to cut the shoreline of the lake into the plywood access hatch cover. Buy a piece of frosted pebbled window glass the size of the access hatch, and build a detailed lake *bottom* into the opening in the plywood. Then cover the lake with the glass. Install the hatch and lake and build the upper scenery so that it matches the lake bottom and shoreline, like the glass lake on the Sverna Park Model Railroad Club layout in Figure 2–10 (also shown in the color section). When you remove the lake, the shoreline remains, so the details along the shore must be fairly robust to withstand accidental buffeting.

You can also camouflage the access hatch with a river shoreline, following the same technique, if you can locate the access hatch or the river so that a big river bend coincides with one or two edges of the access hatch. A dam across the river could camouflage another edge of the hatch, or you could place a highway or dirt-road bridge across the river to coincide with an edge of the access hatch. The river bend and another side of the access hatch could also disappear behind a small hill.

Fig. 2–10 A frosted-glass lake, such as this one on the Sverna Park Model Railroad Club layout, can drop downward to reveal a hidden access hole.

The same suggestions for a river apply to using a paved road as the boundary for an access hatch. Figure 2–11 shows in cross-section how the edge of a river must be shaped through the scenery and benchwork so that the access hatch can drop downward. LeRoy Thompson used the edge of a road and the ballasted back edge of a track to disguise the edges of his lift-up access hatch in Figure 2–12.

A vertical rock cliff is an excellent camouflage for one or two edges of any access hole if the cliff's bottom edge, where it joins the access hatch, is just steep enough so that the joint is not visible from the

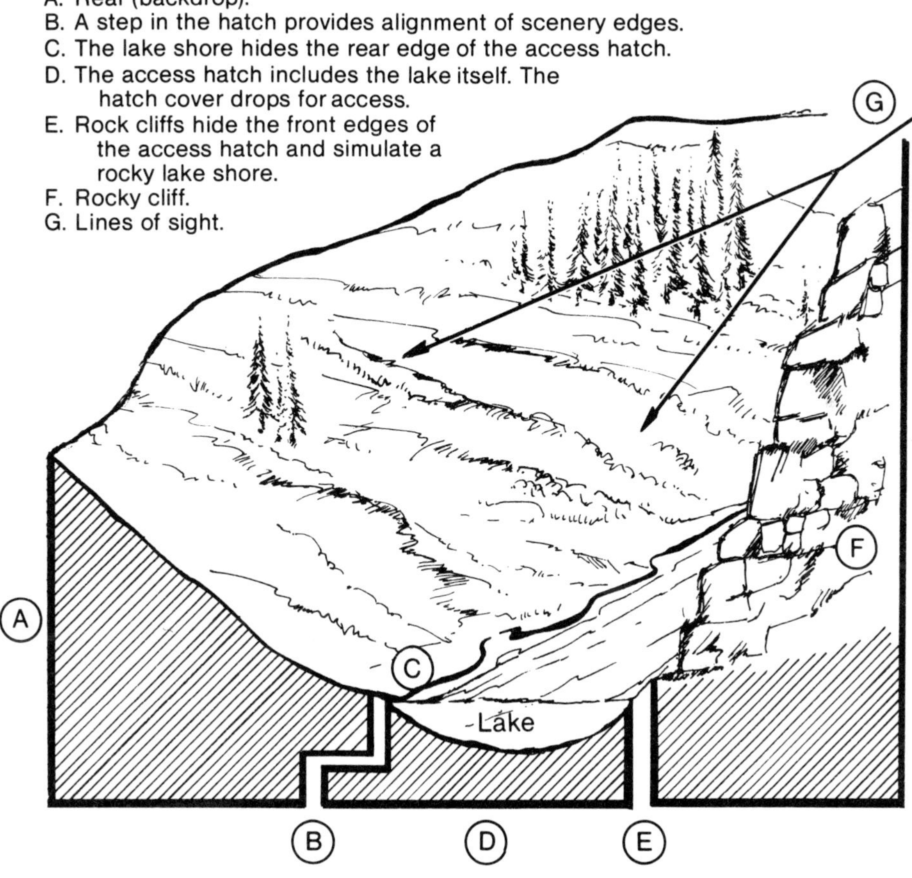

Fig. 2–11 The viewer's line of sight across any access hatch determines the technique used to disguise its edges and cover.

Fig. 2–12 The desert-covered access hatch on LeRoy Thompson's HO-scale layout has hinged 2 × 2 boards to support the hatch cover.

viewing aisle. Most of the downsloping cliff can be visible from the aisle so just the last vertical inch or so seems to disappear over the edges. A few matching rocks on the hatch itself will help carry on the deception that the cliff continues.

Perhaps the most effective camouflage even for the most obvious edge of an access hatch is ground foam in medium and coarse grinds. Simply sprinkle the foam along the edge and expand the line to a wave or patched design so that the straight edge of the hatch is not repeated in the foam texture. Glue the foam in place to both the hatch and the scenery with bonding agent (see Reference Card 12) and allow it to dry for at least two days before moving the access hatch. Then remove the hatch and let it tear the foam in a rough, jagged line. When you replace the hatch, the rough foam-textured edge should disappear in the shadows and highlights of the foam. You may have to add just a sprinkling of foam in some places along the edge (and apply more Bonding Agent) if the joint is still visible.

Chapter 3

Railroad Rights-of-Way, Streets, and Roads

The focal point of most model railroad scenery is the track itself, and not just the rails and ties, but the twenty-scale feet or so on either side of the track known as the right-of-way. This stretch of land is deeded to the railroad and maintained by it. The right-of-way extends beyond the ballast and includes bridges, culverts, earthen fills that lead to bridges, or cuts that lead to tunnels. Model railroaders, always cramped for space, often cram so much "scenery" into their limited space that they ignore the railroad right-of-way, the most important scenic element of all.

Ballast and Borrow Pits

The term *borrow pit* is commonly associated with highway construction. The borrow pit is the ditch beside many state highways that was left when the dirt to elevate the highway itself was "borrowed" from the land. Nearly all full-size railroad mainlines—including the quaint two-foot narrow gauge railroads in Maine, the three-footers in Colorado, and the shortlines such as the Sierra Railway and the Ma & Pa—have both ballast and borrow pits. The railroads usually called borrow pits "drainage ditches," and these ditches are as important a part of railroad tracks as the ties or ballast.

The dimensions in Figure 3–2 provide an adequate-width right-of-way for standard or narrow-gauge model railroads. Most narrow-gauge railroads and branchlines and even standard-gauge mainlines built before about 1905 did not have the luxury of the embankment shoulder (C in Fig. 3–2). The ballast would tumble down the sides of the em-

Fig. 3–1 Mike Bishop's N-scale right-of-way has fresh ballast on the main line, old ballast on the siding, and two sets of power lines.

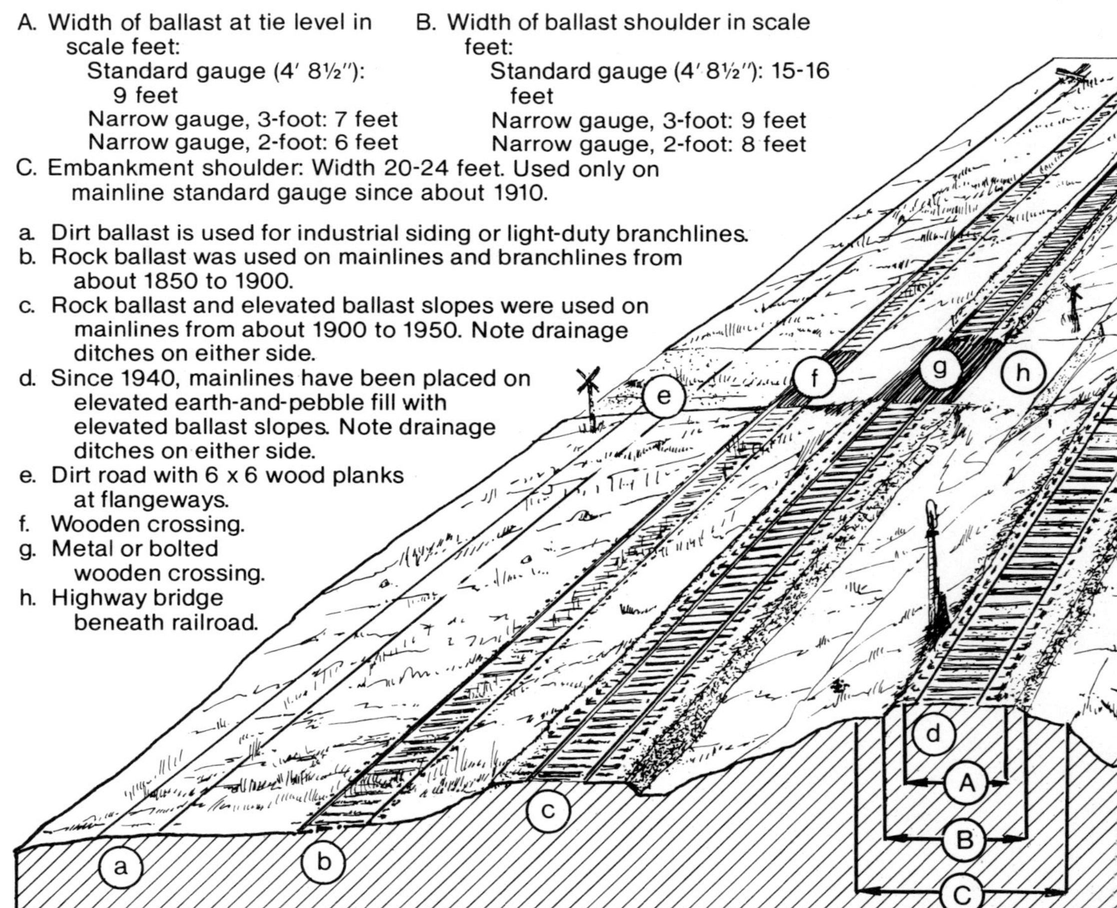

Fig. 3–2 A cross-section of a railroad right-of-way shows the different shapes and sizes of roadbeds and crossings.

bankment on these types of rights-of-way. This lack of control over the position of the ballast shoulder (B) was what prompted the railroads to add additional ballast to the embankments to produce the shoulder in C.

The four tracks in Figure 3–2 show the differences between mainline and branchline trackage and ballast, embankments, drainage ditches. The reason for the difference in the construction of the surfaces beneath the tracks was simply one of cost, and of the need for heavy- or light-duty roadbeds to match the intended traffic. A spur track to an industry that ships relatively light materials doesn't have to be as strong as one that supports hundred-car unit trains of 100-ton loads per car seven times a day. The width and style of roadbed construction also varied with the period; one of the most amazing aspects of the Union Pacific's abandoned roadbed near Promonotory, Utah, which dates back to about 1870, is its extremely narrow width—barely a foot or so wider than the ends of the ties.

The four types of roadbeds in Figure 3–2 can be used to help define the type of railroad you want to duplicate in miniature. It would be unusual, for example, to have seen a Shay-type logging locomotive working along well-ballasted and drained track like that on the far right. And it would have been impossible for a Union Pacific "Big Boy" steam locomotive to operate over either of the tracks on the left. If your model railroad includes mainline, older sidings, branchlines, *and* industrial tracks, you might want to duplicate all four kinds of roadbeds on your layout.

Modeling the Right-of-Way

To provide a place for drainage ditches and for potential fills and valleys, elevate the roadbed and the subroadbed supports for the tracks at least 3 inches above the framework for the benchwork. If you use egg-crate or "open-grid" benchwork (Fig. 3–3, left), elevating the trackwork is a simple task. The tabletop should be cut away so that the edges of the right-of-way extend only as far as they would on the real railroad. Use the widths in Figure 3–2 as a guide. The subroadbed and roadbed for a narrow-gauge railroad or a turn-of-the-century standard-gauge line would need to be only about two-thirds as wide as those for a modern railroad.

Once you have built the subroadbed, roadbed, track, and ties (ballast can be installed *after* the scenery), you can proceed with cuts, fills, or tunnels.

Fig. 3–3 Ed Patrone has begun to texture his scenery (right); the open-grid benchwork is still visible on the left.

Planning for Bridges and Trestles

With open-grid construction, you can actually complete most of the scenery work before installing bridges. Steve Hatch of Railway Engineering used open-grid construction for the HO-scale layout in Figure 3–4, with a $\frac{1}{4}$-inch plywood subbase, $\frac{1}{8}$-inch Upsom board (a cardboardlike wallboard sold through lumber dealers), and hand-spiked rails on wooden ties. He completed the basic scenery shape and textures and installed wood supports that later would be covered with sheet plastic bricks and stones to simulate the bridge abutments. The bridge on the middle-level curve has been started by replacing the plywood and Upsom board over the span with longer wooden bridge ties and the wood supports that will later become the deck of a wooden trestle. The actual trestle bents will be cut to fit the distance from the

Fig. 3–4 Steve Hatch shaped and textured his scenery before adding the bridges and trestles on his HO-scale railroad.

bottom of the deck to the surface of the scenery. The long upper curve will be spanned with a long trestle to connect two wood truss bridges— one over the now-dry riverbed and the other over the middle- and lower-level tracks. The upper-level track has not yet been laid.

Albert Hetzel used the more common method of installing model bridges: He lifted the portion of track for the bridge and attached it to the bridge itself. Only the bare wood backings for the bridge abutments are in place (Fig. 3–5). The actual scenery shape beneath the bridge has not been installed yet. The track extends beyond the length of the bridge to leave space on each end for the guardrails that rail-

Fig. 3–5 Albert Hetzel completed this deck-girder bridge and its track before finishing the scenery that will go below the bridge. The bridge is a Campbell kit.

roads use inside of each track's running rails to prevent derailed stock from jumping the track and falling off the bridge.

The precise alignment of the rails in every direction is as critical at bridges as at other rail joins. Actually, it's risky to use Steve Hatch's approach of completing the scenery before installing the bridges. But the risk is minimized if you use the portion of track to be removed for the bridge as the pattern for the track that will rest on the bridge itself. Extend the rails (or the rails and ties, if you are using plastic ties on ready-laid track) at least two inches beyond the ends of the bridge, as Albert Hetzel did. By using the shell-style scenery-shaping technique, with Hydrocal plaster and paper towels, it's relatively easy to break or cut through the plaster to install bridge abutments or to provide wooden supports for the bottoms of trestle bents.

Ed Patrone's HO-scale layout is an extension of the basic diorama theory. Ed's layout is larger than average—filling a 14 × 15-foot room (see Figs. 3–3 and 3–6)—but he has planned it carefully, spending the extra time to make the scenery as important as the railroad. The

Fig. 3–6 This 4-foot-long wooden trestle rests on a ½-inch plywood riverbed on Ed Patrone's HO-scale layout.

tracks, for example, are located so that there is enough space for realistic hill slopes of 45 degrees or less between the upper and lower tracks.

Ed's planning also included the location of bridges, those over tracks and those that would span later highways or roads and streams or rivers. It would be difficult to add a 4-foot-long replica of a wooden trestle (Fig. 3–6) to any model railroad if the trestle was not part of the plan. Ed not only planned for the trestle, but he actually built the trestle first with wooden supports for the bases of the end trestle bents. He did *not*, however, glue the trestle to the bents, he removed the trestle, leaving the wooden supports for all the bases of the trestle bents. The plaster-and-paper-towel scenery was then installed *around* each bent's wooden support to leave the exposed wooden top of each bent clear to ensure the proper fit with the base of the trestle. The scenery was painted and textured and the trestle was replaced, but each bent was held in place only with a thin bead of rubber cement

Fig. 3–7 A 1 × 4 scrap elevates the foot of the center bridge abutment on Sy Simonton's layout while the riverbed plaster is completed.

so that the trestle could be removed again if the layout was dismantled or altered. Finally, loose sifted dirt and ground foam were dusted around the tops of the wooden supports for the trestle bents to bury the bottom of the bent and the exposed supporting board.

The center twenty or so bents are all the same height, so they simply rested on a flat piece of $\frac{1}{2}$-inch plywood that was firmly attached to the benchwork. Again, the actual places where the trestle bents were to touch the plywood "bottom" of the ravine were covered with plaster, dirt, and texturing only *after* the completed trestle was in place with its rubber-cement mounting. When the scenery was complete, the lower portion of the trestle was painted with a wash of about 20 parts water and 1 part Polly S paint to match the color of the scenery. This coat blended the trestle into the scenery and gave it a weathered look of splashed mud and wind-borne dust.

Tunnels

The interior walls and the portals of tunnels must be installed *before* the mountains that cover them are constructed. Sy Simonton's O-scale wooden tunnel portals and interior were assembled with an open top so that he could reach over the walls and into the top of the hollow mountain to rerail cars or locomotives (Fig. 3–8). He also installed small lights on either end of the tunnel for inspecting the track inside in the case of derailments. Similar construction techniques can be used for the interior walls of brick or stone tunnels. For tunnels cut through rock, place a wrinkled aluminum-foil mold over the tracks and shape it with wadded-up newspapers. Cover the foil with a layer of Hydrocal-soaked paper towels, then apply two additional layers. When the plaster sets, remove the newspapers and foil and paint the interior. For inside larger mountains and hence longer tunnels, the interior can be made removable by simply resting it over the track that will go inside. If maintenance or derail problems occur, the plaster shell-style liner can easily be removed.

Streets and Roads

Streets and roads, like the railroad tracks and rivers, are the "thread" that leads viewers to feel that there is a link between the real world and the model. The street or road can lend a romantic atmosphere to

Fig. 3–8 Sy Simonton finished the inside of this wooden tunnel before he started the 0-scale mountain and cuts leading to it.

a scene by winding out of sight behind a hill (or ending abruptly at the edge of the table or diorama) to suggest that real people come and go along it. Models of such vehicular paths are some of the most challenging aspects of scenery building because everyone *thinks* he knows exactly what a street or road looks like. Once again, refer to the real world or to color photographs when you re-create streets and roads.

Planning for Traffic

Few model railroaders have the foresight to include the path of a winding road when they plan mountain scenery. With few exceptions, the real railroads' rights-of-way are paralleled by roads or highways.

Even the narrow-gauge railroads that challenged the Rocky Mountains and the Sierras were often located just a few dozen or a few hundred feet down the mountainside from the original stage or toll road into the wilderness (Fig. 3–9). A model railroad scene usually looks more credible with a road near the tracks than without one. But the scenery must be planned so that the cuts and fills for the roads are included in the space allocation for the scenery.

It is not necessary to support roads with the sturdy benchwork and subroadbed needed to support the tracks. The support for the roads can be made from corrugated cardboard supported by the same wadded-up newspapers that support the shapes of the mountains. However, you must prop sticks or other cardboard strips beneath the roads to be certain they are nearly level side to side. Take care with uphill grades for roads; they usually climb no more than twice as steeply as the railroad. There is no need to make roads as wide as they are in the real world; as shown in Chapter 8, the art of "selective compression" can be used to make a scale 16-foot-wide road pass as a replica of a real one that is 24 feet wide.

Dirt Roads

Dirt roads must be planned just as carefully as paved roads. You don't have to worry about dirt roads on level farmland, but there must be space for at least a scale 8-foot-wide level space from side to side for a dirt road through mountainsides. Using real dirt on a dirt road is the most realistic medium. Dirt selection and preparation techniques in Chapter 5 give the finest possible grit for the road's surface.

Most dirt roads and virtually all paved roads have a "borrow" or drainage pit on either side of the road on both level ground and through any cuts. You can build up the road with a thin layer of plaster and scrape the surface of the still-wet plaster smooth with a scrap of 1 × 4 wood. Keep the road as level and smooth as possible. Scale-model ruts and ridges can be created with just a few extra granules of dirt. Use the Soaking Agent and Bonding Agent on Reference Cards 11 and 12 in Chapter 8 to hold the loose dirt in place. The only special technique that is needed to make the difference between plain dirt and a dirt road is evidence of traffic. You can build up a center ridge with a strip of dirt spread through the notch of a file card folded in half. Spread the pile of dirt down the center of the road with your fingertip. Allow the Bonding Agent to dry for at least a week, then scrub the

Fig. 3–9 The dirt road dominates this scene of the Slim Gauge Guild.

road with a coarse typing eraser or a track-cleaning eraser such as a "Bright Boy" (Fig. 3–10). The eraser will smooth out the road by moving it *only* in the direction of "traffic," and it will lighten the color of the dirt slightly.

Railroad Crossings

With the exception of modern rubberized inserts, nearly all railroad crossings are either wooden planks placed between the rails or continuations of the concrete or blacktop pavement. The rubberized crossings can be simulated with pieces of plain plastic cut into scale-size 2 × 8-foot blocks and glued between the rails to the tops of the ties. The plastic must be thick enough to bring the roadway *almost* to the tops of the ties. To be safe, any model railroad crossing should be between .005 and .010 inches (the thickness of paper or a business

Fig. 3–10 Real dirt is the best material for simulating dirt roads, but the wear surfaces must be rubbed with a hard rubber eraser.

card) *below* the tops of the ties so that coupler pins and gears cannot accidentally drag on the crossing. Use wood strips to simulate real wood crossings.

If you want superdetails for either type of crossing, buy some of the smallest nut-bolt-washer castings from a model railroad dealer (Grandt makes them in plastic) and cement them to the crossing to simulate exposed bolt heads. The rubberized modern crossings and the planks weather to a similar shade of dark gray. Touch the bolt heads with dabs of aluminum-colored paint where car tires wear them and Polly S Boxcar Red to simulate rust where tires do not travel across the crossing.

If you want to simulate a concrete- or blacktop-paved crossing, buy some twine or rope at a hardware or macramé craft store that is about the same size as the rail on your model track. Lay a piece of the twine or rope tightly against the inside edges of both rails (Fig. 3–11). You can hold the twine in place with a scale railroad spike or two if nec-

Fig. 3–11 Bury twine along the insides of the rails when shaping plaster roads, and remove the twine (as shown) after the plaster hardens.

essary. Leave at least two inches of loose twine beyond the crossing to serve as a "handle." You can now spread molding plaster or plaster of paris down the road and across the crossing to bury temporarily both the twine and the rails. Use a scrap of wood to scrape the still-wet plaster so that it is just barely below the tops of the rails. Let the plaster harden, then immediately and carefully pull out the twine to leave the flangeway clearances inside each rail. This same technique works especially well for duplicating trackwork laid in city streets.

Concrete and Blacktop Roads

Concrete and blacktop roads can be made in any scale from 1/220 to about 1/16. Blacktop roads are usually rougher, but the roughness should *not* be modeled in the Celluclay or in any other rough texture. A three-inch-wide flat-ended putty knife or spatula can be used to apply and spread the plaster. The plaster for roads should be mixed with more plaster than usual to yield a mixture that is just a bit softer than fresh bread dough or child's modeling clay. It is wise, too, to color the water before mixing the plaster to give a medium-gray color to the dried road surface.

For city streets and other level paved areas, tack a "curb" of $\frac{1}{16}$-inch-square stripwood to the edges of the road. Fill the area between the strips with plaster and use the tops of the strips as a straight, even guide for a block of wood to spread and level the top of the road. If the final surface is still rough, wrap some medium-grit sandpaper around a scrap of 2 × 4 lumber to make a sanding block, then sand the surface perfectly level. The wood strips can then be removed. If you are adding curbs, the strips can remain. For curbs, tack down slightly larger square strips of wood to provide the proper curb height for the scale of your model. Use curb-height strips (plus the $\frac{1}{16}$-inch road thickness) for both the front and back edges of the curbs and repeat the road-building process to finish the curbs.

The only difference between a model of a concrete road and a model of a blacktop road should be color (see Reference Card 3). On country roads, however, the blacktop usually crumbles into the sand beside the road, leaving slightly wavy edges. You can duplicate this effect simply by sanding the exposed edges of the plaster slightly (and/or the $\frac{1}{16}$-inch wood-edge strips). The dirt techniques in Chapter 5 apply to the edges of paved country roads as well.

Most concrete country roads are edged with several feet of blacktop

Paved Road Colors

Material to be Simulated	Polly S Paint	Glidden Interior Latex Paint
Blacktop (Tar or Macadam)		
Undercoat gray	Grimy Black PF14	Night Owl
Fresh tar wash	Reefer Gray PR12	Big Ben
Weathered tar wash	Equipment Gray PF12	Pewter
Fresh gravel wash	Dust PR3	1 part Cobweb 1 part Night Owl

Note: The wash mixture should be between 9 and 19 parts water to 1 part paint.

Material to be Simulated	Polly S Paint	Glidden Interior Latex Paint
Concrete		
Weathered concrete	Dust PR3	1 part Cobweb 1 part Night Owl
Typical concrete	Concrete PR82	Smoked Pearl
Fresh concrete	Equipment Gray PF12	Pewter

Note: At least two "concrete" colors should be blended in each section of concrete. Scrub on the darker color with a fine-pore sponge as a wash or 9 parts water to 1 part color.

and a sand shoulder, so the road edges for either concrete or blacktop are almost identical. Before you paint this kind of road, mask off the concrete with masking tape using a ruler to guide your hand while finishing and painting the shoulders. Remove the tape and paint and stain the concrete.

Cracks in the Road

Concrete and blacktop roads crack with age and both are patched with beads of tar. Concrete roads, however, have additional perfectly straight cracks that are also filled with tar about every twenty feet or so. These straight tar seams are expansion joints that allow the concrete to expand and contract with a minimum of cracking. Some sidewalks have similar lines, placed about every three feet, to provide a decorative effect that helps disguise the actual tar-filled expansion joints. You can simulate either type of crack on blacktop and concrete roads by slicing lightly into the surface with a sharp hobby knife. Use a steel ruler to guide the knife. With a paint brush, flow a trace of India ink into the cracks, and before the ink can dry wipe away the excess with a tissue. Apply only about 6 inches of ink at a time so that

Fig. 3–12 Outline the cracks and seams in plaster/concrete roads and sidewalks with ink-filled knife cuts, as Tom Knapp did in this scene.

Fig. 3–13 The realism of this blacktop road is heightened with Creative Screen Process decals and street signs.

you can wipe it away before it dries. The ink will remain *only* in the cracks. You can use a wash of 19 parts water to 1 part Polly S black paint to highlight the texture of concrete streets and curbs and a similar wash of lighter gray to "weather" blacktop streets. The fine sand that collects in the gutters, center, and edges of blacktop roads is easiest to simulate by spraying on a wash of gravel-colored Polly S with an airbrush. Simulate the similar effect of rubber tire wear on blacktop roads with a wash of black along the traveled areas.

Street Markings and Signs

Creative Screen Process makes street signs and decals for on-the-street markings in HO scale. Since there is no standard size for such markings, they can also be used for N and O scale if the spacing of the letters is adjusted. This firm also makes decals for white and yellow lines. Several brands of model-airplane decals offer stripes that are the proper width for any scale center lines. When you apply the decals, use at least a dozen coatings of decal solvent, such as Krasel's "Micro Sol," over the decal to force it to adhere to the rough plaster. Spray the decal-covered street with Testors "Dullcote" to blend the decal into the street.

Chapter 4

Mountains, Valleys, Rocks, and Cliffs

Nearly every individual scenic feature for dioramas is available ready-built or as a simple kit. The textures and trees described in Chapters 5 and 6 are all available ready to use. Firms like Preiser and Faller even make sheets of plastic that can be used virtually as is to produce lakes, swamps, and marshes. When it comes to creating complete hillsides, mountains, and valleys, however, the Styrofoam or expanded polystyrene products from firms like Bachmann and Life-Like are strictly for the amateur. This chapter, then, is the one area of scenery where you *must* do it yourself. The thin-shell scenery technique, using Hydrocal plaster and industrial-grade paper towels, is just about as simple and easy a method as you'll find. Industrial-grade paper towels are available through janitorial supply firms and industrial drug companies. Buy them in brown or off-white, not blue.

Reference Card 4 lists the most important tools and containers that you will need. You may have many of these on hand already, but purchase some extra ones, since the chemicals used for scenery could contaminate them.

Paper and Plaster Scenery

The thin-shell scenery technique illustrated later in the chapter is recommended for several reasons, including simplicity and relatively low cost. It also allows you a "preview" of the completed scenery before you mix any plaster. The thin-shell scenery shapes are made from industrial-grade paper towels (household paper towels tear too easily when soaked in wet plaster) and the brand of plaster called Hydrocal. Hydrocal was designed for making sturdy castings that

A. Loose ground foam and sifted dirt will hide the seam when the layout is reassembled.
B. Scenery, plaster, and track is cut between the plywood contour boards with a saber saw.
C. Thin-shell self-supporting precolored plaster scenery base made from Hydrocal and paper towels.

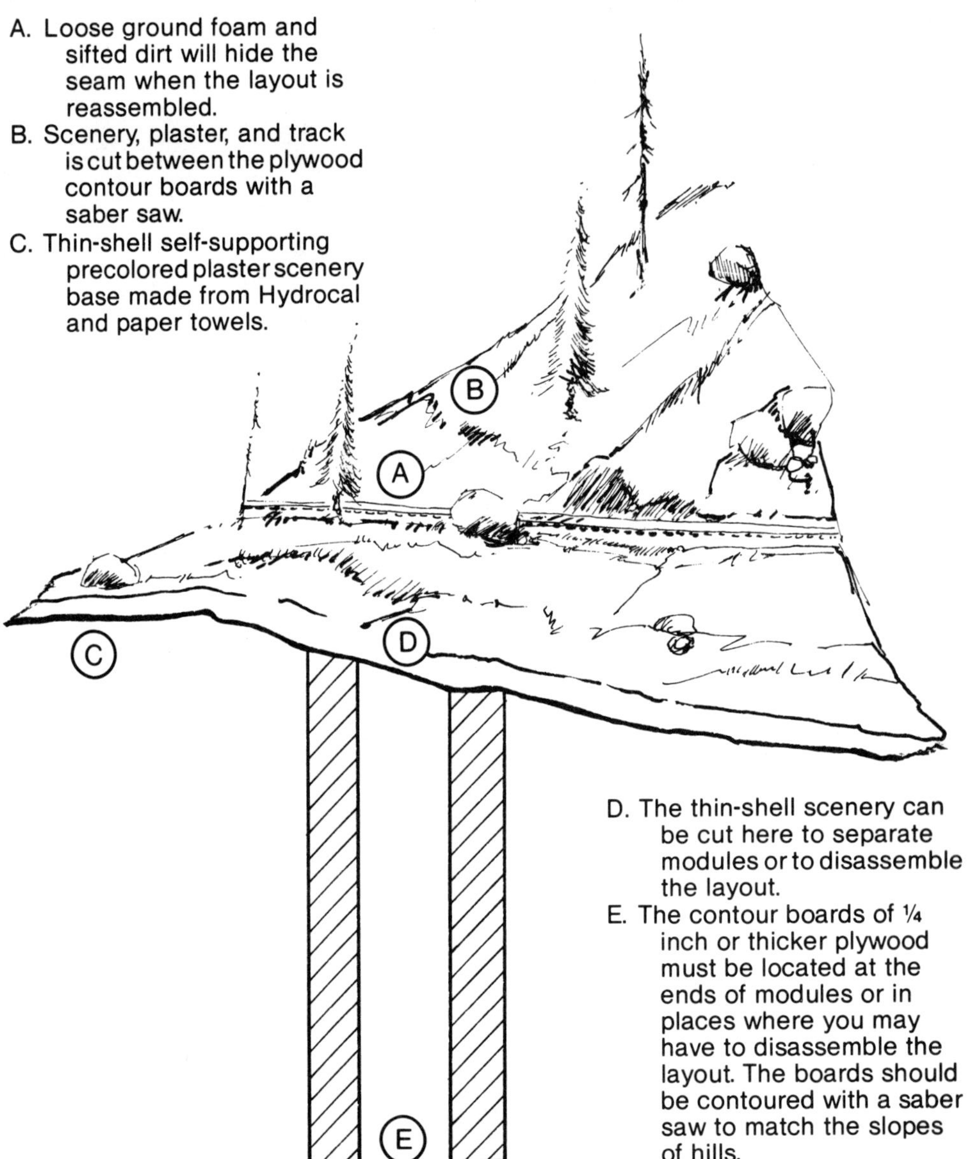

D. The thin-shell scenery can be cut here to separate modules or to disassemble the layout.
E. The contour boards of ¼ inch or thicker plywood must be located at the ends of modules or in places where you may have to disassemble the layout. The boards should be contoured with a saber saw to match the slopes of hills.

Fig. 4–1 A cutaway section of thin-shell scenery. The two cutaway plywood contour boards (E) are needed only if the layout is cut to make it movable or for use as modular layout sections.

Tools and Equipment, Materials, and Containers for Simple Scenery

Basic Tools and Equipment

Clothespins
Scissors
Staple gun
Spatula or palette knife
Ice-cream sticks and tongue
    depressors
Measuring spoon
Pyrex measuring cup
Steel ruler
Plastic basting syringe
Glass eye droppers
Awl or ice pick
Serrated kitchen knife
Butter knife

Pin vise
Magnet
Tweezers
Pump-style spray bottle for
    misting plants
Inexpensive paint brushes, sizes
    0, 00, 0000, 2, $\frac{1}{4}''$, and $\frac{1}{2}''$
Steel-bristle brush
Fine-pore sponge
Coarse-pore sponge
Rubber kitchen spatula
Floquil's Polly S "Standard"
    color chart
Floquil's Polly S "Model

Railroad" color chart
Glidden's "Spred Satin" color
    charts
Flour sieve with screen-door-
    size screen
Tea strainer
Noch-brand "electrostatic"
    applicator for flocking
Emery paper, 600 grit
Single-edge razor blades
X-Acto or Zona-brand razor saw
Masking tape
Airbrush, air pressure regulator,
    and air compressor (optional)

Basic Materials

Floquil's Polly S paints
Glidden's "Spred Satin"
    interior latex paints, or
    equivalent brand
Celluclay or Gold Seal's Modern
    Mâché
Hydrocal, molding plaster, and
    plaster of paris
Ground polyurethane foam
Artist's matte medium

Artist's gloss medium
Aluminum foil
Newspapers
Industrial-grade paper towels
    (brown or white)
Cotton gauze
Alcohol, denatured or isopropryl
Liquid dishwashing detergent
Macramé polypropylene twine
Ultra-Glo or Envirotex epoxy
    resin

Pearl-white fingernail polish
Mason's cement
Fabric dyes
Woodland Scenics' "Foliage
    Material"
Electrical wire, 10 gauge
Steel wire, 30 gauge
Plastic clothesline
Plastic wrap (like Saran Wrap)
(continued)

Basic Containers

Pyrex glass mixing tray for plaster
Flexible plastic mixing bowls for texture materials
5-gallon plastic buckets with snap-on lids (one for water, one for plaster of paris or molding plaster, and one for Hydrocal plaster)
Plastic or glass jars and coffee cans with lids for storing textures, powdered colors, leftover precolored plaster, liquid dyes, washes, and specially mixed colors
Baggies or Ziploc plastic bags for storing textures

would be nearly as hard as rock when dry; the material, in fact, is similar to alabaster when it dries. Any lumberyard can order Hydrocal for you. The paper towels are soaked in a cream-consistency mixture of Hydrocal and draped over the scenery shapes to form *all* the scenery surfaces. The Hydrocal-soaked paper towels are strong enough to be self-supporting after the plaster sets if two or three layers are used. But the actual shapes of the mountains and valleys must be built up with another material before applying the Hydrocal-soaked towels. You could use the traditional wire-screen-and-board approach to shaping the scenery, but there is no need for such substantial supports. Wadded-up newspapers provide ample support for the towels until the plaster sets. The newspapers can then be removed.

Newspaper Mock-ups of Full-Size Scenery

The interesting advantage of using the thin-shell scenery technique is that the supports for the mountains and valleys are actually full-size mock-ups. The mock-ups must remain in place until the Hydrocal sets. If you don't like the shape of the scenery, you can change it before

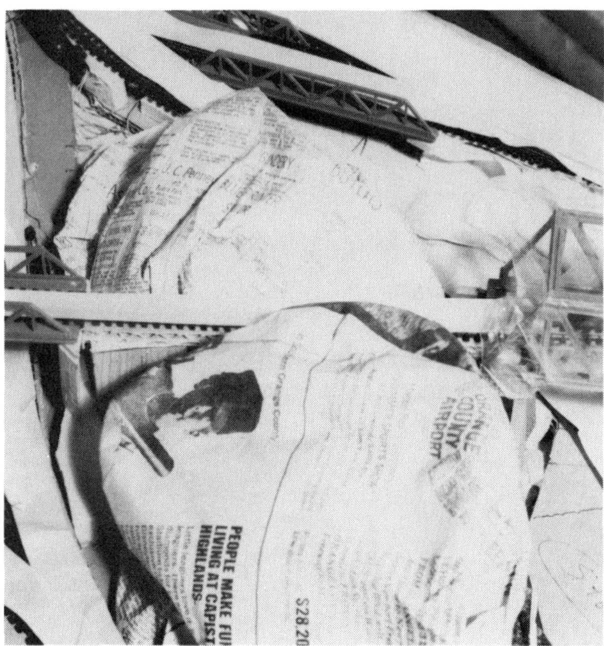

Fig. 4–2 Water-sprayed sheets of newspaper or paper towels can be used to cover the wadded-up newspapers to define the shapes of the hills.

you apply the Hydrocal-soaked paper towels, or you can wait until the Hydrocal sets and break away portions of the scenery to patch in your corrections. Thus you don't have to gamble on how the final shapes of the scenery will look on the layout. If you are using open-grid benchwork, you may temporarily have to nail some scraps of corrugated cardboard boxes beneath the layout to keep the wadded-up newspapers from falling to the floor. You may also have to nail some similar supports or some scraps of wood trim, lath, or 1 × 1 wood strips to the edges of the table to keep the piles of wadded-up paper towels in place. If the towels are too springy, spray them with water. You may be able to visualize the shape of the scenery better if you cover it with a single layer of dry paper towels. The printing and shadows of the newspapers can be confusing. The layer of plain paper towels, either brown industrial grade or white household towels, will provide a better image of the actual shapes.

Profile Boards

When the mountains and valleys reach the back and front edges of the table, you are faced with the problem of supporting them. Do *not* attempt to bring all the scenery to the level of the tabletop. Some areas should rise far above the table edge, while others will require that you cut into the table edge to provide space for deeper valleys. If you use open-grid benchwork (see Fig. 3–3), you won't actually have to cut into the benchwork. The newspaper mock-ups show you precisely where the mountains and valleys will be at the front and rear of the table. In effect, the table edges slice right through the scenery to produce a profile of the mountain or valley at that particular point. Many modelers make a rough-edged cut in a board to finish the edge of the table. The boards are called "profile boards" because they trace the profile of the scenery at that point (Fig. 4–3).

Profile boards can be cut from $\frac{1}{8}$-inch thick plywood or from a hardboard like Masonite. Seal the boards thoroughly with latex paint before applying the plaster scenery. If you prefer a rocklike effect along the edges of the table, nail or screw the profile boards to the *inside* edges of the table. The Hydrocal and plaster can be draped over the profile boards and pulled right down to the table edges. The resulting vertical "cliff" can then be detailed to represent rocks. You can decide whether the cliff faces are supposed to represent the strata revealed

Fig. 4–3 George Booth used Masonite profile boards on his simple 4 × 18-inch diorama. This gave him the freedom to model both a cut (right) and a fill.

when someone cut the access aisle through the scenery or just a rock cliff complete with some weeds and perhaps a small rivulet or waterfall.

Mixing Plaster for Thin-Shell Scenery

If you enjoyed playing with mud pies as a child, you will probably enjoy working with plaster. You cannot work with plaster without getting it up to your wrists, if not your elbows. One solution is to purchase some elbow-length rubber gloves or one of those rub-on coatings that mechanics use. And always wear old clothes. The conventional system of American measures is listed on Reference Card 5 to help you keep track of how much of everything you need. Measure what you use and make a note of it so that you can repeat your results. Use a Pyrex mixing pan for plaster because it is easier to clean after the plaster sets than conventional glass. As an alternate, use flexible plastic pans, but keep in mind that some of the dust from the set plaster will remain in the pores of the plastic.

Always, always, add plaster to water. This method prevents the

Liquid and Level Bulk Measures

1 teaspoon (1 tsp.) = 1.33 fluid drams

1 tablespoon (1 tbsp.) = 3 teaspoon

2 tablespoons (2 tbsp.) = 1 fluid ounce

4 fluid ounces = $\frac{1}{2}$ cup

8 fluid ounces = 1 cup

16 fluid ounces = 1 pint

32 fluid ounces = 1 quart

128 fluid ounces = 1 gallon

Mixing Molding Plaster, Plaster of Paris, or Hydrocal

1. Measure and mix thoroughly:
   2 cups cold water
   1 tablespoon dry powdered mason's cement *or* Rit liquid clothing dye

2. Mix thoroughly:
   1 measure of retarder as indicated on container *or* 1 tablespoon vinegar.

3. Mix thoroughly:
   approximately 2 cups molding plaster or plaster of paris

4. Stir thoroughly while pouring powdered plaster into water until mixture reaches the consistency of whipping cream.

   Note: Use Pyrex-type glass mixing containers and flexible cooking spatulas for mixing ingredients.

plaster from forming into hardened piles in the pan. Of course, you must continue to stir as you add the plaster to the water. Also you should color the water, rather than adding powdered color to the plaster. Precoloring the plaster is extremely important: If you use white plaster, it will be nearly impossible to color every nook and cranny, and patches of white will be visible from various viewing angles. Even the master model railroader and scenery caricature expert John Allen made that mistake on his first two railroads. The snowy white patches of plaster looked like snow, a disturbing effect on the summer scenes.

Plaster-Setting Retardants

Don't be afraid to experiment with retardants to delay the setting time of the Hydrocal or, when you install rock castings, to delay the setting time of the plaster of paris or molding plaster. You know that you need a retardant when you find that the plaster in your mixing tray begins to harden before you are finished. Actually, you have two choices: Mix less plaster or Hydrocal, or mix the same amount and add some retardant. There are two extremes here: You may mix as little as a two-ounce paper-cupful of molding plaster if, like Dick Shurberg, you want to hand-carve rockwork, or you may want to mix as much as a half-gallon of Hydrocal if you want to cover a large mountainside in just one evening.

If you must retard the setting time of Hydrocal, you have only one alternative: Buy the U.S. Gypsum (the makers of Hydrocal) retarder that is designed especially for use with Hydrocal. Any other kind might weaken the set Hydrocal. For conventional plasters, such as molding plaster or plaster of paris (almost identical plasters), use either white household vinegar or hydrous citric acid from a large drugstore or chemical dealer. The amount of retarder is something you must experiment with; it can range from as little as $\frac{1}{2}$ ounce per 128 ounces to as much as $\frac{1}{2}$ ounce per 8 ounces, depending on your climatic conditions and just how long you must delay the setting time. In general, the more retarder you use, the weaker the plaster will be after it sets.

Making Mountains

It's now time to get up to your elbows in plaster. Start with a quart of water and however much coloring and Hydrocal is necessary to make a mixture about the consistency of whipping cream. Tear the paper towels into strips about 4 × 12 inches until you have enough to cover at least two square yards. Do this *before* mixing the plaster. Dip the torn paper towels into the colored Hydrocal mix and drape them over your newspaper scenery (Fig. 4–4). Overlap at least half of each towel (Fig. 4–5). Repeat the dipping and overlapping process until you run out of the first mix of Hydrocal.

Keep a gallon bucket of water on hand so that you can immediately rinse out the pan and the mixing spatula before making a second batch. Mix this batch exactly like the first, and cover the area you just finished with a second overlapping layer of Hydrocal-soaked towels. You will then have at least three (usually four) layers of Hydrocal and paper towels in every area of the scenery. This is the minimum for self-supporting scenery. If you are covering only a square foot or so of open space, you may be able to get by with just the first two overlapping layers. Cover every inch of scenery, even those areas that will become rock cliffs. Remember, though, to keep the Hydrocal layer far

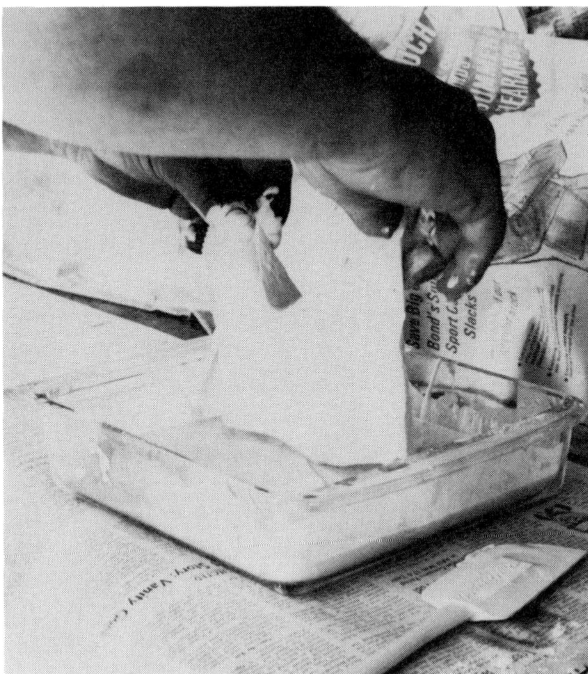

Fig. 4–4 Dip and thoroughly soak the paper towels in the creamy Hydrocal.

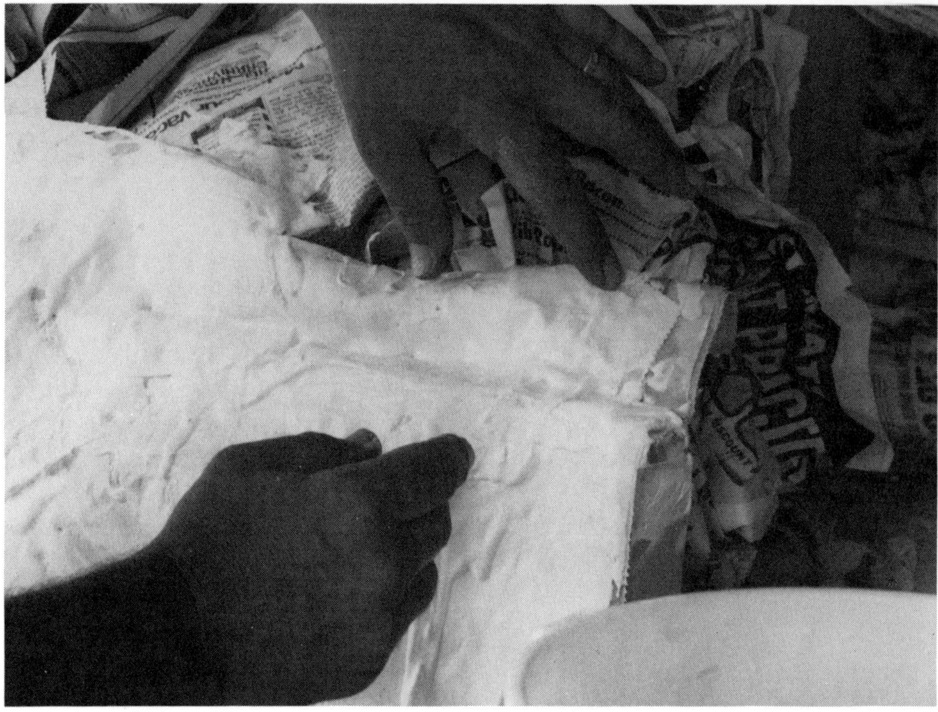

Fig. 4–5 Overlap the towels by about half to prevent any thin areas or holes.

enough away from the tracks or proposed structures to leave space for rocks.

It should be obvious by now that working with plaster is a messy business. You must protect the track and any structures against splashing plaster. The track itself can be covered with a ¾-inch strip of masking tape for N- or HO-scale track. This is one reason why many modelers ballast their track only *after* the scenery and coloring and textures are complete. It's easier not to have to worry about other scenery up to the edges of the ties than to try to protect the ballasted edges all the way through the scenery process. If some bridges must be left in place, they can be covered with plastic wrap or Baggies. Saran Wrap is best for protecting tunnel portals because it can be tucked in close to areas that will receive plasterwork (Fig. 4–6).

Use pieces of flat plywood or hardboard cut to the size of any building sites. Include enough space for adjacent roads or parking lots.

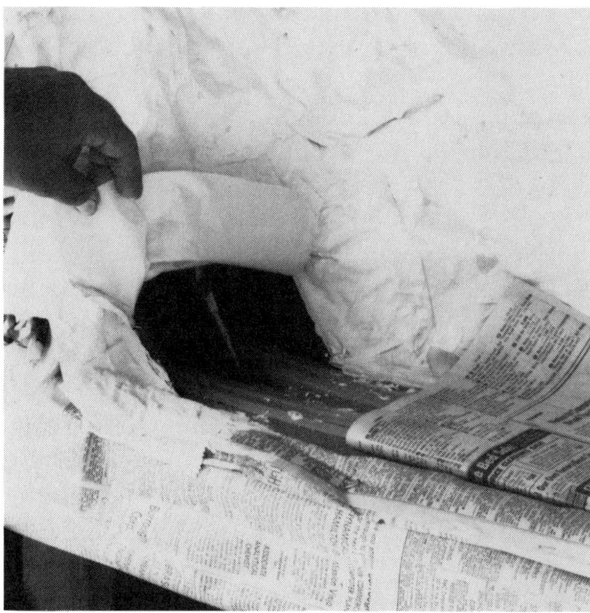

Fig. 4–6 Protect tunnel portals with plastic wrap (like Saran Wrap) before covering them with the Hydrocal-soaked towels.

These pieces can be supported by wadded-up newspapers or nailed to the track as subroadbed. Roads can be constructed from corrugated cardboard to give them a flat surface, and that surface can be coated either with plaster or Hydrocal until the final layer of plaster or Celluclay is applied. Unless the foundation of a building is on sloping land, such as a mine, remove the building during the Hydrocal application process. The base of the building can be "buried" later during the application of dirt or other scenic textures. If you must cover the base of a mine, trestle, or other structure with Hydrocal, cover the rest of the structure or bridge with Saran Wrap. The entire work area of course should be covered with six or more layers of newspapers to make cleaning up easier. You may also want to mask the edges of the benchwork with masking tape and paper towels. If you know in advance that the cleanup will be easy, you'll find that working with Hydrocal or plaster is actually fun.

Rocks and Cliffs

Nothing looks more like a real rock than a real rock. However, a real rock seldom looks like a scale-model rock. The texture of the rock may be perfect, but its color is made up of sand-size particles that are the size of boulders in a 1/87-scale environment. What you need is the best of both worlds—the texture of real rock and the proper colors for a miniature scene. You also must be certain that you are using the real rocks in their proper places so that they do form cliffs or outcroppings.

Model railroaders have developed a five-step technique for duplicating the texture of real rocks and their color. (1) A latex rubber mold is made of a portion of a real rock (or a real piece of coal or driftwood); (2) a mixture of powdered plaster, color, and water is poured into the mold; (3) the plaster is slapped against the scenery so that the "rock" can bond to the scenery and bend slightly to conform to its shape; (4) the rubber mold is peeled away the moment the plaster just begins to harden; and (5) the rock is stained with a dark brown, reddish brown, or gray stain to accent the cracks and crevices. That's all there is to it. Color-Rite and other firms even make the rock molds for those who want to skip this step. For rocks in small dioramas or those that would go to the edge of the layout, you can use the weathering technique in Chapter 10 to produce more color variations. You will also want to texture the lower edges of any cliff with small pebbles or talus made from broken-up leftover plaster colored to match the rock cliffs.

Rubber Molds for Rock Castings

The process of making a latex rubber mold to create plaster castings goes back nearly to the 1940s. Latex is a special liquid that vulcanizes, or cures, at room temperature, and it is sometimes referred to as RTV (Room Temperature Vulcanizing). There are several industrial compounds of it, but those suitable for modelers are sold by craft supply stores (for casting plaster or clay figures in homemade molds) and by many model railroad shops under the "Mountains in Minutes" label. Follow the instructions on the label of the liquid latex or RTV liquid.

You will need a small roll of cotton gauze to reinforce the mold and a spray can of silicone lubricant to serve as a mold-release agent. Select a suitably textured rock, piece of broken coal, or driftwood (see Chapter 2). Your molds should range in size from a minimum of about 4 × 4 inches to a maximum of about 9 × 12 inches, so you won't need a very large rock or piece of coal as your master pattern. Also, you can overlap and rotate the plaster castings to produce as large or as small a rock cliff as you need. Remember that there is no substitute for a photograph of the real rock cliff to give you a general idea of the texture and relative positions of the fissures and cracks in the real rock face. Most modelers are satisfied with no more than a half-dozen different rock molds taken from several different textures of real rocks.

To make the latex or RTV mold, spray the area you want to duplicate on the real rock with several thick coats of silicone lubricant. Let it dry for at least an hour. Use a disposable paint brush or wooden tongue depressor to smooth a layer of the latex or RTV about $\frac{1}{16}$ inch thick over the portion of the real rock. Let this first layer cure completely, then apply a second, thinner layer and cover it with two pieces of gauze. The gauze should sink into part of the still-wet latex or RTV. Next, cover the gauze with another $\frac{1}{16}$ inch or so of latex or RTV, and let those last two applications cure completely. Repeat the latex/gauze/latex process at least once more for molds smaller than 6 × 6 inches, and add a third layer for molds larger than about 6 × 6 inches. The gauze, embedded in the several layers, reinforces the mold so that it won't rip when you remove it from the later applications of plaster.

Fig. 4–7 Coat the mold with a few layers of latex paint before pressing on the first layer of gauze.

When the latex has cured completely, gently peel the mold away from the rock. Small chunks of the latex or RTV will be caught and torn away where they were embedded in the cracks and fissures. Don't worry about them because they won't noticeably affect your model rock textures. Let the mold dry for three or four days before using it again. Store all your rock molds in a box large enough to hold some of those pesky Styrofoam "peanuts" or discs used for packing. The molds will weaken and tear if they are folded.

Although Hydrocal can be used for rock casting, it is too hard and dense to approximate a realistic texture when stains and paints are applied. Molding plaster is available at lumber retailers. If the bags are too large for your needs, substitute the nearly identical (but more costly) plaster of paris sold in hardware stores. You will want the castings to cure relatively rapidly, so you probably won't need to use any retarder for rock casting. You might want to use retarder if you intend to carve your own rocks or if you intend to carve the castings to blend them into an adjacent hand-carved area. Be sure to mix some powdered color or dye into the water (see Reference Card 6) so that the *dry* plaster looks like colored chalk. You will want to add some stains and highlights to the rock, so don't make the plaster as dark as you would for earth surfaces.

Fill the mold only with about $\frac{1}{4}$ inch of plaster. Try to judge the amount by pouring the water into the mold first to see how much is needed, then pour it into the mixing pan. This mixture can be just a bit thicker than that used for thin-shell scenery. The plaster should be just thin enough so that you can pour it from the mixing pan without any lumps. If you make it too thick, it won't reach the tiny detail areas of the mold. If you make it too thin, you will have to wait too long for it to cure, and you will spill the plaster on your way from the pouring area to the cliff.

Instant-Setting Plaster/Water Mixture

It may take as long as 15 minutes for the plaster-filled rock mold to harden from the mudlike state to the firm state which enables you to peel the mold away, leaving the plaster "rock" firmly attached to the Hydrocal mountain. You can reduce that time by about one-third if you prepare a special water mixture, as the Slim Gauge Guild discovered, *before* mixing the powdered plaster for rocks to be cast in latex molds.

Add about 2 tablespoons of raw powdered plaster to a quart of water; thoroughly color the water so that it looks like milk. Let the water and plaster mix sit, after a thorough stirring, for 20 minutes to allow the plaster to cure. This plaster-treated water apparently provides a catalytic action when the bulk of the powdered plaster is mixed in, reducing the curing time to about one-third that of the usual mixes. (This is the reason it's wise to clean any plaster or Hydrocal mixing containers thoroughly after each batch; the leftover plaster acts much like the treated water I've just described to accelerate the curing process.) With some practice, you'll find that the treated water will allow you to slap a plaster rock of muddy consistency onto the mountains, then hold the latex mold around that rock only about 3 minutes before the plaster is hard enough to retain its shape when you pull the latex mold away. Do remember, too, to pre-wet the Hydrocal mountain with plain water (or detergent water) so the mountain does not leach all the water from the plaster rock before the plaster has time to cure. When applying several (or several dozen) plaster rocks to a single area, the adjacent rocks should also be sprayed with water just before the fresh plaster-filled mold is applied, so the new rock texture will adhere.

Casting Directly on the Mountain

The process goes very rapidly, once you understand the timing that's involved. The procedure is to fill the latex or RTV mold with about $\frac{1}{4}$ to $\frac{1}{2}$ inch of very soupy plaster. Hold the mold and shake and wiggle it to help release any trapped air bubbles while you wait for the plaster barely to begin to cure. At that exact moment, you literally slap the mold and plaster up against the cliff (see Fig. 4–8). The plaster will adhere to the cliffside better if you first spray the area thoroughly with water and about 4 drops of dishwashing detergent per pint of water. Push the mold firmly against the cliff so that the plaster will conform to the shape of your Hydrocal cliff. Don't worry about distorting the shapes of the rocks inside the mold. You want the mold only for texture. The cliff behind the plaster provides the shape.

Hold the mold right there until you can just feel the plaster harden. (It will also begin to give off some heat, but you may not be able to feel it.) It takes some practice, because the sooner you can remove the mold, the easier it will be to get it off without tearing or breaking off the smallest details. If you remove it too soon, the plaster will run and the detail will be ruined. If you do pull the mold off too soon,

Fig. 4–8 Members of the Slim Gauge Guild slap one of thousands of still-wet plaster rock molds and plaster against a mountainside.

immediately scrape as much of the plaster away as you can, spray the area with more water, and try again. The adjacent areas of rock should overlap the first by about $\frac{1}{4}$ to 1 inch, so you may want to keep the plaster in the second mold just a bit thinner (about $\frac{1}{4}$ inch) along the edge that will overlap the first rock casting. Pay attention to any "grain" in the fissures in the mold, and apply the grain at random or keep it parallel to the other castings, depending on the type of real rock you are trying to duplicate.

Throwaway Foil Molds for Rock Castings

The folded and cracked effects of granite and similar types of rocks can be duplicated by using aluminum-foil molds. Cut or tear a piece of foil about 4 × 6 inches. (It's not practical to use pieces larger than about 5 × 10 inches.) Crumple the foil into a tight ball and gently unfold it, then crumple and bend it loosely (see Fig. 4–9). The process of making this kind of mold is exactly the same as that for latex or RTV rubber molds. When the foil mold is peeled away, it will probably tear, so a fresh piece of foil must be used. There are two tricks to the foil-mold process; getting those tight little crumples right, and using the same crumpling technique with each foil mold so that the texture does not vary. Nearly all of the scenery on Lee Nicholas's HO-scale Rio Grande layout (see color section and Fig. 2–1) was made with crumpled-foil molds.

Quick Coloring Tips

Reference Card 7 describes just about every color you will need for rocks, earth, and soil. This chart, and most of the others, is designed for use with various water-base paints. The Polly S color charts are sold for about $2 through hobby dealers, or you can order them directly from Floquil/Polly S. Alternatively, Glidden color-chip charts are available nationally, or match them with another brand of high-

Fig. 4–9 Crumpled aluminum foil can also be used as a mold for casting rocks in plaster.

Earth, Soil, and Rock Colors

Color	Applications	Artist's Acrylics	Polly S Paint	Glidden Interior Latex Paint
Black	Shadows or *dulling* washes only, not as color or wash itself	3 parts Lamp Black 1 part White	Grimy Black PF14	Night Owl
White	Not recommended	—	—	—
Off-white (chalk)	Chalk cliffs, mineral-salt deposits on edges of dried ponds	19 parts White 1 part Burnt Sienna	Antique PF16	Chalk
Light gray	Limestone, some sandstones, cement or concrete	9 parts White 1 part Burnt Sienna	Dust PR3	1 part Cobweb 1 part Night Owl
Medium gray	Limestone, granite, sandstones, cement or concrete	4 parts White 1 part Burnt Sienna	Equipment Gray PF12	Pewter
Gray	granite, basalt, sandstones, fresh or new concrete, blacktop roads	3 parts White 1 part Burnt Sienna	Reefer Gray PR12	Big Ben
Beige or tan (light yellow)	Sandstones, some river sand	3 parts White 1 part Yellow Ochre	Mud PR83	Ponce De León

Note: Artist's Acrylics: Match colors to Polly S color chips by mixing as indicated.

Polly S paint: Floquil's water-base paint matches its military and model railroad paints. Part numbers PF are standard series; part numbers PR are model railroad series. In some cases, a nearly identical color is offered with two part numbers.

Glidden interior latex paint: The names are from the Spred Satin series. These colors closely match Polly S paints and actual soil and rock colors.

(continued)

Earth, Soil, and Rock Colors, *continued*

Color	Applications	Artist's Acrylics	Polly S Paint	Glidden Interior Latex Paint
Beige or tan (medium yellow)	Sandstones, some river sand	1 part White 1 part Yellow Ochre	Sahara Sand PF62	Birch Bark
Beige or tan (dark yellow)	Sandstone, some river sand, shale	9 parts Yellow Ochre 1 part Burnt Sienna	Medium Military Brown PF65	Seville
Beige or tan (Brown)	Sandstone, river sand, shale	9 parts Yellow Ochre 1 part Burnt Umber	Earth PR81	Penuche
Beige or tan (Gray)	Sandstone, river sand, shale	9 parts Yellow Ochre 1 part Black	Desert Light PF63	Caravan
Pink or rose	Sandstone, basalt, granite, sand	8 parts White 1 part Indian Red 1 part Raw Sienna	Heritage Red PF19	Rambling Rose

(continued)

Earth, Soil, and Rock Colors, *continued*

Color	Applications	Artist's Acrylics	Polly S Paint	Glidden Interior Latex Paint
Clay or brick red	Clays, sandstone, sand	4 parts White 1 part Raw Umber	1 part Boxcar Red PR74 1 part Caboose Red PR20	Oxide Red
Reddish brown (Light)	Sandstone, shale	1 part Burnt Sienna 1 part White	Rust PF68 or Rust PR73	Indian Paint
Reddish brown (Medium)	Sandstone, shale	Burnt Sienna	Boxcar Red PR74	Wild Turkey
Rich brown	Sandstone, shale, and farm soil	1 part Burnt Sienna 1 part Burnt Umber	Dirt PR69	Hickory
Dark brown	Mudholes, river deltas, plowed earth	Van Dyke	Roof Brown PR70 or Dark Earth Brown PF64	1 part Hickory 1 part Night Owl

quality latex interior wall paint. The most important element in scenery is color, and these charts are the "key" to locating the correct colors. All of the colors on these charts have actually been matched to rocks, dirt, concrete, blacktop, and sand. *Warning:* Take the color chip charts from Polly S or Glidden outside and match the colors for yourself. You may need to add some white or off-white to any of these color samples to obtain the correct pastel shades according to your lighting conditions.

Use these color chips when mixing powdered colors or fabric dyes with plaster or Hydrocal so that your plaster will be similar to the final scenery colors. The dried plaster will of course be lighter than when it was wet. Mix the colors so that the dried plaster actually will be a few shades lighter than your paint-on earth colors. You can also use these earth colors as "glue" for attaching dirt as well as earth and foliage-colored ground foam textures to nearly all the scenery that is not textured with rock castings (see Chapter 5).

Adding Depth to Rocks

If you added enough color to the water when you mixed the plaster for rock casting, you now have the basic rock color. The color also disguises any chips (or deliberate holes for trees) that might occur later. For most rock faces, the only additional coloring needed will be a simple shading to bring out the texture of the castings and to emphasize any fissures. Apply a wash of about 19 parts water to 1 part paint, and the color will automatically be deposited in the textures and crevices and washed away from the highlights as the water evaporates. Never use black for the wash color; it will create a harsh, unrealistic salt-and-pepper effect. Select a "shadow" color from the same family as your basic rock color, only several shades darker. Use brown (Rich Brown or Dark Brown, from Reference Card 7) to provide the shadows on Beige (brown) rocks. Use Reddish Brown for rocks that are to be beige (reddish brown), and so forth.

For larger cliffs, you can literally flood the plaster by applying the wash with a basting syringe, available in grocery and hardware stores. Smaller rock outcroppings can be shaded by brushing on a darker wash (Fig. 4–10). For close-up detailing, you may want to apply several colors using the weathering techniques in Chapter 10. The Polly S paint mixes for spray-painting with an airbrush (Reference Card 8) will provide professional scenery effects.

Fig. 4–10 If you precolor the plaster for the rock casting, you can apply a darker wash to highlight the cracks and texture.

Retaining Walls and Cliffs

Most model railroaders include far too many rock cliffs in their scenery. Even the brave builders of the narrow-gauge railroads through Colorado's Rockies were forced to bolster the mountains to keep rocks from falling on or out from under the tracks. Consider facing at least one-third of your vertical slopes (any cut, fill, or cliff steeper than about 45 degrees) with a simulated wood, cut stone, or brick retaining wall. Ready-to-use retaining walls are available with proportions suitable for N, HO, and S scale from firms such as A.I.M., Chooch, Color-Rite, and "Mountains in Minutes." If you use these preformed, precolored products, be sure to mask their detailed faces with masking tape to avoid plaster droppings or discoloration from the paints and washes you use for the surrounding scenery.

Quarries, Rubble, and Talus

Perhaps the most difficult scenery feature to capture in miniature is a rock quarry. There is a subtle difference between the way rock is

Polly S Paint Mixes for Airbrush Spray Painting

Thinning Ratio with Water

4 parts Polly S paints
1 part water
4 drops liquid dishwasing detergent per pint of fluid
  Use about 25 pounds per square inch of air pressure.*

Note: For a wash, add 9 parts water (and detergent) to the paint/water mixture.

Thinning Ratio with Denatured Alcohol

3 parts Polly S paints
1 part denatured alcohol
  Use about 15 pounds per square inch of air pressure.*

Caution: Alcohol is extremely toxic. Spray it only in a well-ventilated area and wear a mask. Do *not* use isopropyl alcohol, which may contain glycerine or other additives that can retard the setting of the paint.

*Some airbrushes demand slightly more or less pressure, so experiment before painting the final model. Clean the airbrush immediately after use. Acrylic paints, like Polly S, dry rapidly and can clog the airbrush.

Fig. 4–11 Richard Zinn's HO-scale diorama depicts the Rio Grande Southern's Ophir, Colorado, station and log retaining wall.

removed from a quarry and the way it is blasted from a rock cut for a railroad right-of-way. The type of stone being quarried can also make an incredible difference in the appearance of the quarry walls. There is almost no similarity among marble, flagstone, and sand quarries. Open-pit mines fall into the same category. Try to visit a quarry, or find color photographs of one. Or obtain a sample of the type of stone being quarried to use as your model. In many cases the quarried stone

Fig. 4–12 Dave Riggles carved these steps in plaster. A similar, polyfoam stone wall
with steps is made by "Mountains in Minutes."

is several shades *lighter* than the surrounding natural cliff faces. The
natural faces appear to be "wet" examples of the "dry" colors of the
quarried stone. In some instances, the colors are the same.

Remember to add plenty of "rubble," smaller chips and stones that
have dropped to the bottom of any cuttings. The leftover colored plaster from the rock cliff can be placed in a cloth bag and crushed into
scale-size (3- to 24-inch "square") chunks of rock. Color the rubble
with a wash of the same color used to highlight the cliff faces. When
rocks are washed from the cliff faces by nature (usually, by glacial
movement) it is called *talus*. Part of the realism of the Slim Gauge
Guild's scenery stems from its wise use of talus.

Featherweight Scenery

Making lightweight scenery may seem like one of the most difficult modeling challenges, but it can be done successfully with some unusual shaping and texturing techniques. The major purpose of featherweight scenery is to reduce the weight of dioramas and the typical 2 × 4-foot model railroad modules. The diorama or module must be strong enough to be moved without bending or racking (shifting from a rectangle to a diamond shape). The modular layout specifications in Volume 3 of *The Model Railroading Handbook* must be used for a modular railroad. If you are building a diorama or a small model railroad only for home use, the heavy benchwork can be avoided by simply making the base of the diorama or module from a one-inch-thick piece of styrene or urethane foam, such as that used for home insulation. The lightweight concept also applies to the scenery. Unfortunately, plaster or Hydrocal cannot be made light and strong enough to resist cracking. Using styrene or urethane foam will keep the weight to a minimum.

Contour Modeling for Lightweight Hills

The contour method of modeling hills is the one used on the U.S. Geological Survey's topographic maps. When the above-sea-level elevation lines are converted into three dimensions, a stair-stepped model similar to that in Figure 4–13 results. For some architectural and topographic models, this type of contour modeling is enough. For most models, though, the vertical slopes of the contours should be blended into the hillsides and cliffs. Thanks to the easy-cutting nature of styrene and urethane foam, it's relatively simple to shape the slopes with a hollow router blade, like the X-Acto blade and knife in Figures 4–14 and 4–15, or with a serrated paring knife. The slopes can be smoothed with a steel-bristle brush (Figure 4–16) and painted with a mixture of paint and ground walnut shells (Fig. 4–17) or covered with a thin layer of plaster of paris or molding plaster. The rocks can be cast from latex or RTV rubber molds, but use the liquid polyfoam made by "Mountains in Minutes" to retain the lightweight concept. Alternatively, premolded polyfoam rocks from "Mountains in Minutes" can be used for those textures.

Fig. 4–13 The shape of these hills follows the same contours and elevations of U.S. Geological Survey topographic maps.

Styrene and Urethane Foam Sheets

The type of lightweight cellular plastic boards used for home insulation are usually suitable for the lightweight scenery shown here. There are two types of foam boards: those made from expanded styrene, like the soft white foam in inexpensive ice chests, and the somewhat harder and more powdery expanded urethane, similar to the material used by "Mountains in Minutes." Urethane foam is less flexible, so there's less chance that the scenery will crack if the module or diorama is accidentally flexed or bumped.

Both materials produce dust when cut, sawed, or sanded, so always work outdoors. The dust can be toxic, so wear gloves and a face mask or respirator. The panels can be cut with a serrated paring knife or a hacksaw blade held with a gloved hand. Many glues will dissolve

Fig. 4–14 Shave off the square corners of the urethane or styrene contours with an X-Acto wood router blade.

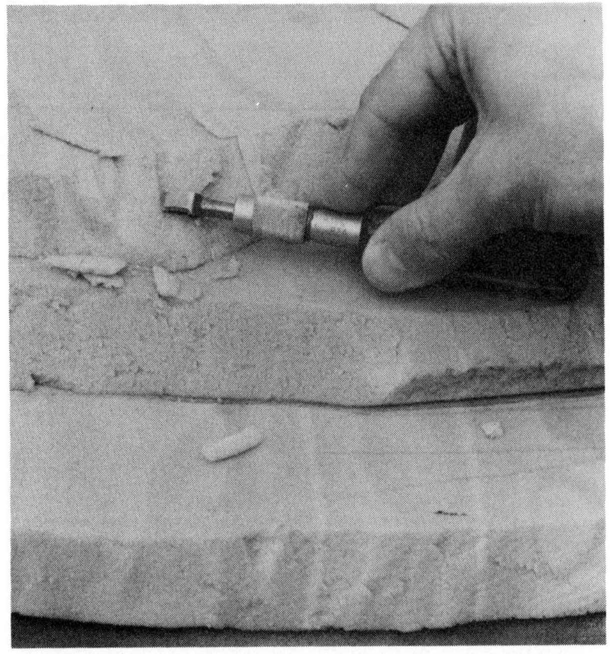

Fig. 4–15 If you use expanded foam panels for the base, small rivers and valleys can be cut into the base with the X-Acto router blade.

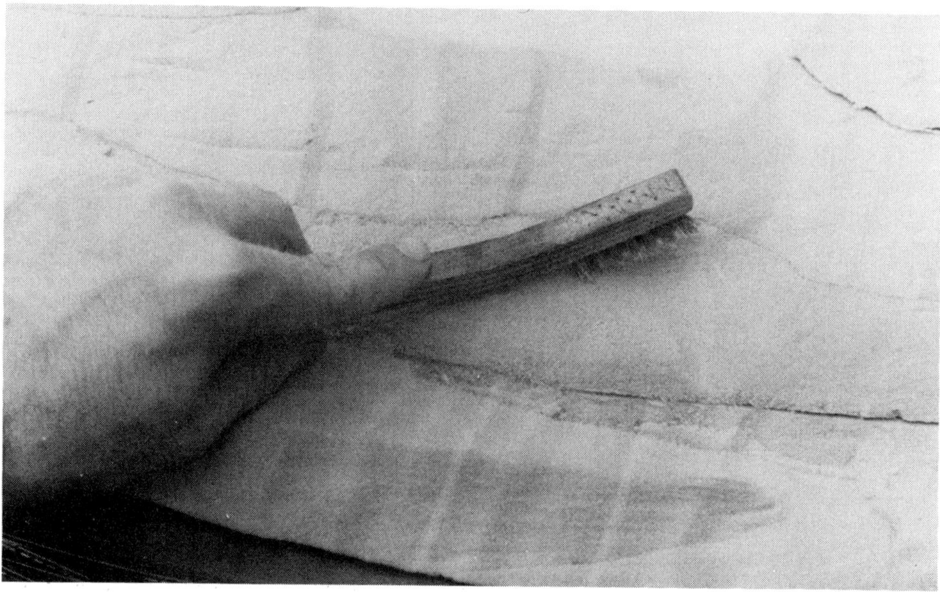

Fig. 4–16 The final shapes are smoothed with a steel-bristle brush.

Fig. 4–17 A mixture of latex wall paint and ground walnut shells provides basic "earth."

urethane or styrene foam; wall-panel adhesive, usually sold in cartridges for inexpensive caulking guns, works best to cement the foam layers together. Water-base contact cement also works well. Whatever you use, try it on a scrap of foam first. All of the low-odor, water-base texturing and bonding formulas in the Reference Cards will work well with the foam.

Familiarize yourself with the contour technique before cutting the foam panels. Compare the contour lines on the map to the hillside so that you can see why the lines of a steep slope are spaced more closely together than a gentle slope. You can remove material from the *inside* of hills or mountains when you cut the contours in the foam panels to save weight, to make the material go farther (the cutouts from the lowest slopes can form the smaller contours for the peaks), and to provide access. Backpacking shops usually supply U.S. Geological Survey topographic maps for the local area.

Shaping the Foam Hills

With the contour technique, the only additional shaping that is required is to bevel the corner from one contour so that it matches the size of the contours immediately above and below it. Use a paring knife, X-Acto router blades and knife handles (Figs. 4–14 and 4–15), or a hacksaw blade. If you are going to add cast urethane foam rocks and cliffs, you may have to trim an extra half-inch or so away from the actual contours to make room for the thickness of the foam castings. The final shaping of the more gentle slopes can be done with a steel-bristle brush (Fig. 4–16). Remember that the open pores of the foam will be exposed with this technique, so you must seal the surface with a coat of thickened latex paint or plaster. Paint is better because it is less likely to crack.

"Mountains in Minutes" Products

I.S.L.E. Laboratories makes special urethane foam products for model railroaders and diorama builders under the "Mountains in Minutes" label, and they are available through any hobby store. Perhaps the most useful products in this line are the preformed expanded polyfoam rocks, tunnel portals walls, and background building "flats." The detail is fine enough to use even with conventional scenery techniques. "Mountains in Minutes" also makes latex rubber for producing your

Fig. 4–18 Jim Ely used "Mountains in Minutes" preformed polyfoam rock moldings for all the exposed cliffs on this HO-scale module.

own rock castings using either plaster or the firm's two-part polyfoam kit. The polyfoam kit allows you literally to "foam" your own castings or mountains. The foam is similar to that sold in aerosol cans for caulking. It expands to about thirty times its liquid volume, and the result is a smooth-skinned foam with a porous core, similar in texture and rigidity to urethane foam panels. You can cut and shape the finished foam just as you would conventional foam. The material is especially useful for filling in the gaps between plaster or polyfoam rock castings and the preshaped contour scenery. You can also build up a mountain shape using the wadded-up newspaper technique; but instead of covering the shapes with Hydrocal and paper towels, use the liquid polyfoam. The technique takes some practice because you have to get to know what a 30-times expansion means. Obviously, the mountain shapes must be smaller and further from the tracks or structures to leave room for the greater thickness of the polyfoam. You also must know how thick a layer of polyfoam to apply, since the expanded layer should be at least an inch thick to be self-supporting.

The plywood or Masonite hardboard table-edge contour panels are especially important to help support the expanded polyfoam. Once you become experienced, you can even plan the shapes of the polyfoam, as you brush or pour it over the wadded newspaper shapes. For most mountains, plan to remove most of the skin to prevent a lumpy texture. Because the "Mountains in Minutes" technique takes practice, buy one kit just for experimentation. Once you master the technique, however, the system is by far the least messy, the lightest, and the most practical.

Chapter 5

Earth, Weeds, Vines, and Grass

One of the secrets of realistic scenery is to make sure that every square inch of the plaster surface is covered. Even if you are going to cover an area with grass or weeds, the underlying plaster should be colored. The ground that is visible beneath any stands of trees also should be textured to simulate earth (covered with fallen leaves, of course), as well as the surfaces of dirt roads and even the ballast beneath the railroad track. The best earth-texturing process uses water-base paint and water-base glue (the Bonding Agent referred to on Reference Card 12) to minimize odors and to speed up the process so you can apply earth, grass, and weed textures the same night that you install the Celluclay, Hydrocal, or plaster earth shapes. If you want to complete a diorama or a portion of a model in an evening or weekend, you can do so without waiting overnight for the intermediate materials to dry. The advantages of the water-soluble system will become more apparent as you add color and texture to the basic scenery shapes.

Earth Colors and Textures

The chart of earth colors in Chapter 4 (Reference Card 7) provides virtually all the basic hues you might want for any model scene. Use a high-quality latex house paint for *all* scenery work. Obtain Floquil's Polly S color charts and Glidden's "Spred Satin" color chips. If you cannot locate Glidden paints or a brand that matches Glidden's colors, simply purchase the Polly S chart and match any brand of latex wall paint to those colors. You may also want to buy Polly S paints for weathering.

Fig. 5–1 With the exception of rocks, cliffs, and river bottoms, *all* plaster surfaces should be painted and textured for maximum realism.

Use the latex paint as an earth color *and* as a binder for the layers of texture materials (see Reference Card 9). The system works best if you apply the texture *immediately* after the paint and, for thicker layers of texture, the bonding agent immediately after that (see Reference Card 12). All three compounds—the underlying latex paint, the texture materials, and the Bonding Agent—are designed to work with either water or alcohol. Any combination of the formulas in Reference Cards 11, 12, 13, and 14 can be applied in one evening. Larger rocks and taller weeds are, in fact, applied *after* the finer earth textures are in place. The larger, taller "textures" can be applied the same evening, or they can be installed using the Bonding Agent anytime thereafter. Thus this system of creating textures allows you the flexibility to "finish" any given area in a single evening with the option of coming back later to add more superdetails.

Treating, Bonding, and Coloring Real Dirt

Using real dirt to simulate dirt can be one of the most frustrating aspects of modeling scenery. Instead of using real dirt, use fine-grind brown foam, which is a simpler alternative. Woodland Scenics' Numbers 41, 42, and 50 "earth" foam in fine grinds will capture nearly as much of the appearances of real dirt in every application except simulating a well-used dirt road. Woodland Scenics also offers matching shades of a medium-grind foam (Number 60) that can be mixed with the finer grades to produce effects such as forest undergrowth and plowed fields.

The simplest way to simulate dirt is to paint the scenery with an appropriate shade of latex wall paint in a thick coat, sprinkle on the ground foam, wet the foam with Soaking Agent (Reference Card 11), and apply the Bonding Agent (Reference Card 12) with an eye dropper or spray bottle. You may want to cover portions of some areas with various shades of green ground foam and even flocking or other weed textures at the same time you apply the ground foam. In general, the "dirt" and the weeds or grass are applied in that order, but *before* the Soaking Agent and Bonding Agent.

You cannot hope to be successful with real dirt until you test and treat it (see Reference Card 10). A further treatment can prove helpful. Take the dirt that has fallen through the tea-strainer and sift it through a brass plumber's screen with a 100-size sieve. (Hardware stores and

Dirt, Weed, Leaf, and Ground-Cover Textures

Texture	Scenery	Sources of Texture
Dirt	Dirt	Pretest real dirt with a magnet. Do not use if magnetic. Sift through door screen, then through a tea strainer to produce medium and fine particles. (See Reference Card 10.)
Sand	Sand	Pretest real sand and sift as above.
Ground foam	Dirt, sand, weeds, grass, leaves, pine needles	AHM, Bachmann, Life-Like, AMSI, and Woodland Scenics.
Sawdust	Not recommended	Sawdust is suitable only around a scale-model sawmill. For all other applications, use ground foam.
Flocking	Weeds, large pine needles	Precut flocking is available loose for use with an electrostatic dispenser and as preglued sheets. The best colors are made by Preiser, Noch, and Sommerfelt, or cut flocking strands from macramé polypropylene twine.
Cattails	Weeds	The material inside tall cattails is the perfect size, color, and texture for weeds.

(continued)

Dirt, Weed, Leaf, and Ground-Cover Textures

Texture	Scenery	Sources of Texture
Foxtails	Weeds	The Individual bristles of fall foxtails make perfect scale-grass weeds. Some types have an inner core that simulates leafy weeds after the outer "bristles" are removed.
Paper punchings	Leaves	Banks and some Telex machines. The tiny holes used by some smaller banks to cancel checks are often collected in the base of the cancelling machine.
Small stones, rubble, talus	Small stones, rubble, talus at the base of cliffs	Leftover precolored molding plaster, plaster of paris, or Hydrocal. Place the leftovers in a cloth bag and pulverize with a hammer. Small batches of broken plaster can be lightly tinted by soaking them in a 50/50 mix of water and latex paint in the color used to highlight rock cliffs and mountainsides.

Testing Real Dirt for Modeling Suitability

Test 1: Touch dirt with magnet to be certain soil is not magnetic. Discard the dirt if it is.

Test 2: Will dirt sift through a screen-door screen?

Test 3: Will the sifted dirt also sift through a tea strainer (half the gauge of screen-door screen)?

Test 4: Mix dirt with water and spread on metal pan to dry. If it cracks as it dries it is clay and not suitable for scenery.

If all four tests are positive, sift dirt through door screen and store in coffee cans with snap-on lids. Match dirt color to Polly S color chip and label can with source of soil, color, and date.

Note: Dirt will be more pastel than any Polly S color. Mix Polly S dirt colors with 4:1, 9:1, and 19:1 pastel mixes of white and color to provide better color samples than too-dark out-of-the-can colors for in-field soil selection.

Soaking Agent for Ground Cover, Dirt, and Ballast

Isopropyl Alcohol
(Rubbing alcohol from any drugstore)

Seal the base beneath the material with latex wall paint and allow the paint to dry completely.
Flood the area with alcohol.

Note: Alcohol helps to pull the Bonding Agent into the loose particles of dirt, ballast, or ground foam. It can be applied with an eye dropper or with a spray bottle in a well-ventilated area. Test the alcohol on plastic material by soaking a scrap for at least a week to be certain the alcohol does not melt or weaken the plastic.

Water-Soluble/Low Odor Alternate
4 drops liquid dishwashing detergent
1 pint warm water
Mix thoroughly, and apply with eye dropper or spray bottle until puddles of water are visible between grains of ballast, dirt, or ground foam.
Apply Bonding Agent (Reference Card 12).

Bonding Agent for "Loose" Textures

1 part artist's matte medium
3 parts water
4 drops liquid dishwashing detergent per
pint of bonding agent
    Mix thoroughly and apply with an eye
dropper or spray bottle after applying
the soaking agent (Reference Card 11):
Note: Common white glue can be used,
but it is more likely to crack as it
dries, and it is difficult to remove. Artist's matte medium
dries with a flat finish and is
more flexible, so the bonded material can be broken away from
the base with a spatula if you
must later alter the scene. Matte
medium thickens in its container
with age. Dilute it with as much
as 8 parts water to 1 part matte
medium.

Solvent	Disadvantages	Advantages
Water	Will not penetrate smaller gaps between granules of dirt, ballast, and ground foam. More suitable if a wetting agent is added (about 4 drops liquid dishwashing detergent) per pint of water. Can warp cardboard or wood if they are not thoroughly sealed with latex or other waterproof paint.	Easy clean up, no odor, inflammable, inexpensive, and little staining or discoloration.
Isopropyl Alcohol (rubbing alcohol)	Extremely flammable (the flame is nearly colorless), toxic, and relatively expensive. Can stain or discolor surrounding ground foam or other colors. Can warp, bleach, and weaken some plastics Most varieties not suitable as a paint thinner for Polly S or acrylics because they contain glycerin or other oils that prevent proper paint setting.	Soaks into and around just about any size dirt, ballast, or ground-foam granule. Will help pull or leach a water and matte medium solution into the bottom layers of dirt, ballast, or ground foam for better adhesion. Used as a thinner for Polly S and acrylic paints, it allows paint to flow better.
Denatured alcohol	Flammable, toxic, and expensive. Can stain or warp plastics and colors even more sevrely than isopropyl alcohol.	Same as isopropyl alcohol. Lack of glycerin or other oils makes it a better thinner than water and detergent. Allows Polly S and acrylic paints to flow better for more even coverage when applied with an airbrush.

Warning: The Dangers of Working with Alcohol

Denatured alcohol:

Can be used instead of water and detergent solution as a thinner for Polly S and acrylic paints. However, it is extremely toxic and flammable.

Isopropyl alcohol:

Can be used as a wetting agent for bonding dirt, ballast, or ground foam with a mixture of water, detergent, and artist's matte medium. The small amount of glycerin and oils contained in the alcohol are absorbed by the texturing material and don't seem to hinder the bonding of the matte medium. Do not use isopropyl alcohol as a paint thinner. The glycerin and oils prevent proper setting of the paint.

Caution

Never use either type of alcohol unless you are working in a well-ventilated room and wearing a protective mask designed for spray painting. And remember that alcohol has an extremely low flash point, and it burns with a colorless, almost invisible flame.

plumbing supply shops sell the screen.) This dirt can be considered "dust" and too fine for model use. (You can simulate mud by mixing the dust with plaster, adding color to the water when you mix it so that you can be more certain of how the plaster will dry.) After the 100-size sieve, you will have three grades of dirt: (1) the dirt that did not pass through the screen-door screen can be used to simulate medium rocks found along stream or riverbeds; (2) the dirt that passed through the screen-door screen but was caught by the tea strainer can be used for rough forest undergrowth or plowed fields; (3) the dirt that passed through the tea strainer but was caught by the plumber's screen can be used to simulate raw dirt and dirt roads and paths. This real dirt can now be applied using the same techniques for applying ground foam or track ballast. Be particularly careful to match the color of paint used beneath the dirt to the dirt itself so that you don't alter the color excessively.

It is possible to *select* just about any color of real dirt and match it to your rocks by mixing latex paint in the proper color in with the final Bonding Agent. Mix 1 part latex paint, 1 part artist's matte medium, and 8 parts water with 4 drops of dishwashing detergent per pint of bonding agent. Experiment with this technique on a scrap of plywood because some types of real dirt absorb more color than others. You may have to add more paint to the Bonding Agent or use a second application of the colored Bonding Agent.

Simulating Loose Dirt

The trick in a model scene is to capture the loose look of dirt, leaves, or blades of grass but still have all the materials glued down securely so that they cannot accidentally be blown into the tracks, turnouts, and operating mechanisms of the locomotives.

You can make a piece of plywood look like a miniture plot of the earth, but even a simple diorama should have at least a slight variation in the level ground. You can add undulations to the plywood or other flat portion of a scene by spreading on some Celluclay or Modern Mâché as described in Chapter 1. Most surfaces of a model railroad will by now be covered with a layer of thin-shell scenery shapes in paper towels and Hydrocal as described in Chapter 4. The point here is that the textures should be used *only* for texture; if you try to apply a thick enough layer to create shapes as well, you may end up with a heap of ground foam.

Try to limit the thickness of any texture to a fine enough covering so that at least *part* of the earth-colored latex paint is visible *when the scene is viewed from directly overhead.* This "crew-cut" effect will contribute more than any single item to the effectiveness of grass and weeds. If you are trying to duplicate a well-used dirt road or path, you may have to cover the latex paint with about $\frac{1}{32}$ inch of material.

The Five-Step Texturing Process

The surface that you are about to texture must be sealed with a waterproof coat of latex paint. This is important when you are texturing a surface made of molding plaster or plaster of paris because portions of the cured plaster may accept or leach more of the water or solvent than others to produce unwanted texture effects and unpredictable bonding. If you use this method to texture raw plywood, Upsom board, or Homosote, a cardboardlike wallboard favored for model railroad roadbeds, the board will probably warp from all the water. The first step in the texturing process, then, is to paint the surface with latex and let it dry for at least two days. Use the paint full strength from the can, and select a color to match the earth you are modeling.

Latex paint can also be used to tint or shade the dirt and texture materials as well as bond them. Brush on the latex in place of the Bonding Agent for this step. This bonding coat of latex paint should be thinned with an equal amount of water to help increase the drying time and to make the paint go farther. Do *not* thin it more than 1:1. Work with no more than about two square feet of the scenery at a time so that you can apply all the texturing material before the paint dries. For the first texturing process or two, work with only one square foot of surface area. Spread the paint as thick as you can, but don't allow it to run down any slopes. When the entire square foot is covered with latex paint or Bonding Agent, you have completed Step 2.

Step 3 must be completed before the second coat of latex paint begins to dry. Sprinkle the dirt, weed, or grass textures directly onto the still-wet paint. Use a tea strainer (Fig. 5-2), or simply shake the material over the edge of an old cup. If you are applying dirt (whether real dirt or ground foam) and weeds or grass, apply all of the dirt first, then follow up with just enough grass or weed texture to cover

Fig. 5–2 Real dirt, tested as on Reference Card 10, can be applied by shaking it through a tea strainer.

the "dirt." The dirt should still be visible when viewed from directly above—the crew-cut effect.

Step 4 also must be done immediately, before the paint has time to dry. Apply the Bonding Agent to the entire area with an eye dropper if the area is small; use a basting syringe if the area is large (Fig. 5-4). You will want to flood the area so that the artist's matte medium is clearly visible between grains of texture (Fig. 5-5).

Step 5 also must be completed immediately so that the fluids from Steps 2, 4, and 5 can all mix together. Spray the area with the Soaking Agent using the finest mist possible. Trigger-operated spray bottles used for misting plants work best. Apply enough of the Soaking Agent so that the area seems to be more white than texture color. Allow the area to dry for a day or more until the white cast disappears before texturing adjacent areas. Allow the area to dry for at least a week

Fig. 5–3 The techniques used to bond ballast are the same as those used to bond real dirt, ground foam, or any loose material. Spray the loose material with a gentle mist of Soaking Agent, using a pump-type spray bottle. Hold the spray at least a foot away to prevent material from blowing around.

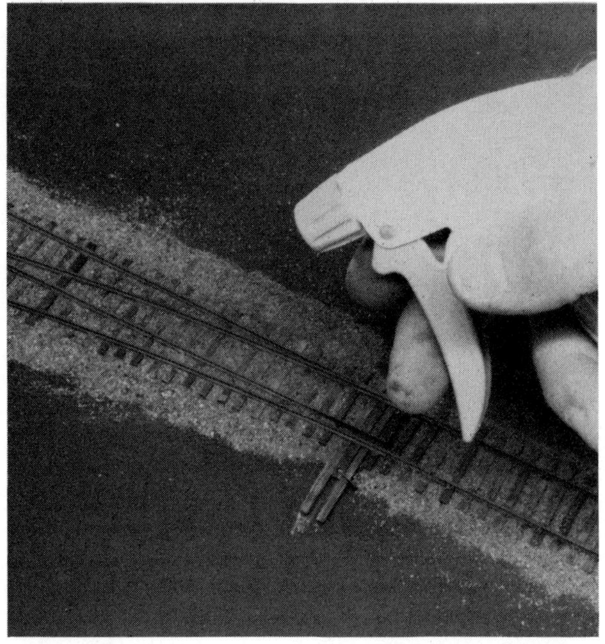

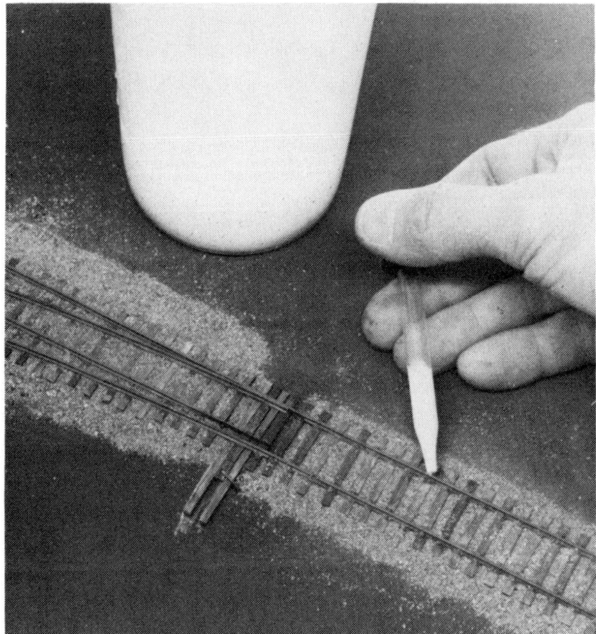

Fig. 5–4 Use an eye dropper (or a basting syringe for larger areas) to apply the Bonding Agent to the well-soaked ballast or texture.

Fig. 5–5 Apply enough Bonding Agent so that the entire textured area is flooded with about equal amounts of Bonding Agent and Soaking Agent. The Bonding Agent will dry clear and flat.

before vacuuming any loose material. Hold a piece of rough cloth such as burlap or hop sacking over the vacuum hose attachment to catch any loose texture for reuse. If you want to simulate plowed furrows in a field or ruts in a muddy road, scrape a comb across the field or a finishing nail head down the road *before* the Bonding Agent dries. The area is now ready for additional weeds, bushes, or flowers.

Weeds, Crops, and Bushes

For purposes of definition, weeds, crops, and bushes are taller than the grasses and low-lying ground covers that can be simulated with the fine or medium grinds of ground foam, but they are smaller than a tree with a visible trunk. There is no single texture better than the various sizes and colors of ground foam to simulate natural growths.

Fig. 5–6 Woodland Scenics' ground-foam was used in this farm scene.

Ground foam reflects light and captures shadows, so it is equally suitable for simulating *clumps* of grass and weeds, pine needles, and leaves of all types.

Using Lichen Moss for Large Weeds and Bushes

The most readily obtainable commercial product for simulating large weeds, bushes, and even the clumps of foliage on deciduous trees is lichen moss. The pretreated moss sold by firms like AHM, Bachmann, Campbell, Faller, Life-Like, Noch, and LaBelle is usually a special finely tipped moss from Norway. This lichen is noted for its fine leaflike ends. Similar moss is available in the woods of Maine and Florida, and a coarser moss grows on the north sides of conifers in the Sierras and Rockies. Unfortunately, even the best lichens do not *look* like leaves. The same is true of sawdust, which always looks like sawdust. Both materials fool the camera, and that's one reason why so much lichen and dyed sawdust is used on model railroads. Use sawdust *only* to duplicate sawdust around a sawmill or timber op-

Large Weeds, Bushes, Tree Foliage, and Twig Textures

Texture	Foliage	Source of Texture
Must Be Textured with Ground Foam or Paper Punchings		
Lichen	Large weeds, bushes, tree foliage	Norwegian lichen sold under AHM, Bachmann, Life-Like, Preiser, Kibri, and Noch labels. Treated with a glycerin solution to prevent crumbling. Domestic lichen is available in nearly every forest from Florida to Maine to the Rockies. Must be treated with the glycerin and dye solution on Reference Card 18. Do not use lichen as is; it is realistic only when covered with traces of ground foam or paper punchings.
Steel wool	Not recommended for model railroads	Slivers can find their way into the magnets of electric motors and cause short circuits. Suitable only for architectural or gaming models. Several grades available in hardware stores. AMSI makes a precolored brown steel wool that does not have to be spray-painted.
Rubberized horse hair	Small bushes, twigs	Used as a packing material and for some upholstery. Some plastic scouring pads are similar in texture, such as 3M's "Scotchbrite" and "Mr. Potts" brand.
Macramé polypropylene twine	Large weeds, bushes, twigs	From craft supply stores. Color-fast light gray/brown shades suitable as is for twigs. A similar material is used for the twigs in AHM, Bachmann, and Life-Like tree kits.
Woodland Scenics' "Foliage Material"	Large weeds, bushes, twigs with foliage, some conifer boughs	Fine-grind foam already glued in place, similar to macramé fiber. Must be pulled apart for the see-through effect of real foliage.

(continued)

Large Weeds, Bushes, Tree Foliage and Twig Textures, *continued*

Texture	Foilage	Source of Texture
Wool felt	Clumps of tall weeds and small bushes	Individual fibers can be brushed from the felt with a steel- or brass-bristled brush. Use as is for some weeds or treat with a trace of ground foam.
Air fern	Weeds, bushes, boughs of some conifers	From flower shops and craft supply shops. A live Kelly green plant, it requires no treatment, but there is no way to alter the color.
Asparagus fern	Boughs of some conifers and some weeds	A live fern that must be cut and treated with the glycerin and dye solution on Reference Card 18.
Peat moss	Weeds and some small bushes	From gardening supply and florist shops. Contains enough natural oil to use as is. Can be spray-painted with latex or acrylic colors.
Caspia, yarrow, spirea and weeds	Weeds, small bushes, deciduous trees, boughs of some conifers	Flowered ends suitable as is for leaves and pine needles in S or O scale. Must be treated with fine-grind foam for N or HO scales. Dried caspia is available from craft and florist shops.

Weed and Foliage Colors

Color	Polly S Paints	Directions

Dark green	1 part
	  Dark Green PR40
	  or Jungle Green PF50
	1 part water
	4 drops detergent per pint
		Hold the weed or foliage material with tweezers and dip it into the color solution. To apply with an airbrush, thin the mixture with 2 parts water to 1 part paint.

Medium green	1 part Grass Green PF51 1 part water 4 drops detergent per pint	

Yellow-green	9 parts
	  Dark Green PR40
	  or Jungle Green PF50
	1 part
	  Earth Yellow PF41
	4 drops detergent per pint	

(continued)

Weed and Foliage Colors, *continued*

Color	Polly S Paints	Directions
Sage green	1 part Avocado PF55 1 part water 4 drops detergent per pint	Hold the weed or foliage material with tweezers and dip it into the color solution. To apply with an airbrush, thin the mixture with 2 parts water to 1 part paint.
Straw brown	1 part Mud PR83 or PF67 1 part water 4 drops detergent per pint	
Straw yellow	1 part Harvest Gold PF42 1 part Mud PF67 or PR83 2 parts water 4 drops detergent per pint	

eration. And whenever you use lichen, cover it with just a trace of fine-grind green foam. There are three stages in making lichen into small weeds, bushes, or foliage on a deciduous tree. Natural lichen must be treated with both a dye (Reference Card 17) and a preservative (Reference Card 18). Commercial lichen has received both of these treatments, although you may want to alter the bright greens with some yellow or other shades of green. The colors on Reference Card 16 can be used if you spray them on with an airbrush. The glycerin-treated, dyed lichen must also be treated with a trace of fine-grind green foam (from **AHM, AMSI, Bachmann, Life-Like,** or **Woodland Scenics**). You have to treat only the visible upper surfaces, so you can merely dip each piece of lichen into a bottle-capful of Bonding Agent (Reference Card 12). Or you can spray the lichen with cemet in an aerosol can, such as 3M's "Sprayment." (Use this product in a well-ventilated area.)

After coating the lichen with Bonding Agent or spray cement, dip it in an open box of ground foam (Fig. 5-7) and set it aside to dry. After the glue dries, pick up the foam-treated pieces and, one at a time, dip the bottom surfaces into the Bonding Agent just before placing the lichen "bushes" into the scene. This foam treatment will allow you to use all of the commercial Norwegian lichen, even the coarse pieces. The coarse pieces can be treated with a mixture of medium- and fine-grind foam to produce a variation on the more common lichen-and-foam weeds, bushes, or tree foliage. Use rubberized horse hair or unwoven macramé fiber as a variation on the texture of the lichen (see Reference Card 15).

Sagebrush, Chaparral, and Mesquite

Foam-treated lichen can be used to simulate wild plants by selecting the correct shade of ground foam or spraying the lichen with one of the colors on Reference Card 16. For sagebrush, chaparral, and mesquite, which have only a small branch structure visible, use one of the gray or gray-brown shades of lichen for the plant. Allow the ground foam to represent *all* the foliage. With this technique, follow the same lichen-treatment steps. The procedure is quick, and you can cover several square yards of scale-model hillsides with sagebrush in a single evening. Trim each piece of lichen, rubberized horse hair, or macramé fiber to scale size before applying the ground foam.

Color Dyes for Ground-Foam Foliage

Use conventional fabric dyes sold in grocery and variety stores, such as Rit, Putnam, and Tintex powdered dyes.

Measure and mix dye in hot water exactly as outlined on package. To dye paper punchings, use isopropyl alcohol in place of water. Do not heat the alcohol.

Suggested Colors
Olive green
Light green
Dark green
Forest green
Jade green
Kelly green
Goldenrod (orange-yellow)
Yellow

When dyeing ground foam or paper punchings, watch for two changes that will occur during the process: (1) the colors will turn several shades lighter as the dyed material dries, and (2) each succeeding batch of dyed material will be several shades lighter than the previous batch. After several batches have been dyed, the dye solution will still appear to contain as much color as it did in the beginning, but the material will accept only a trace of the dye. When the dye is exhausted, add another package or two following the instructions on the package.

If you mix two or more shades of green and/or yellow, use the same brand for all color mixes; do not mix different brands of dye. When the dyed material is dry, store it in Ziploc plastic bags or jars. Label the bags or jars with the date and the colors used so that you can match the colors again.

Preserving Solution for Lichen and Other Domestic Mosses

For processing a maximum of three gallons of moss (by volume, not weight):

Mix thoroughly:
2 gallons water
1 gallon glycerin
1 package medium green Rit, Putnam, or Tintex powdered dye

Heat mixture to boiling and allow to cool for five minutes.

Submerge the moss in a container and soak it overnight.

Wring out moss by hand. Wear rubber gloves.

Spread moss one-layer deep over newspapers and allow to dry completely.

Portions of the moss can be sprayed with or dipped in the Polly S colors on Reference Card 16 for variety.

When coloring more than three gallons of moss, use a light, medium, and dark green or yellow dye from Reference Card 16 to match the foliage you are duplicating. Process about one-third of the batch using the formula above. The processing will remove some of the glycerin and most of the dye. To replenish the glycerin, add another quart and package of dye. Use light green (or yellow) for the first batch, medium green for the second batch, and dark green for the final batch. Each fresh solution must be heated to boiling and cooled for five minutes, and the moss allowed to soak overnight.

Fig. 5–7 Put the finely ground foam into an old kit box or bowl, then dip the lichen into the Bonding Agent and foam.

Using Real Weeds

Modelers have been searching for natural weeds and other plants to simulate foliage on their model railroads and dioramas for decades. The problem has always been to find a plant in scale size. It's a particularly difficult problem in the common scales used by model railroaders and diorama builders, especially the scales between 1/220 and 1/40 (see Fig. 1–4). Actually, there is nothing in nature fine enough to simulate individual leaves or blades of grass, so it's best to use fine-grind foam on the treated tips of lichen. If you are building a diorama in a scale between 1/4 and 1/8, you may find a natural weed or plant that can be used nearly as is. Only the medium to coarse grinds of ground foam are suitable for these larger scales. Some of the coniferous tree textures in Chapter 6 that are suitable for smaller scales can be used to simulate leaves in 1/4 or larger scales.

When it comes to real weeds, there are a few that can be used for almost any scale. The common weed known as foxtail has individual strands on its seed tips (Fig. 5–8) that can be pulled free with tweezers

Fig. 5–8 Foxtails, or this type of barley grass, make effective weeds on T. R. Smith's HO-scale layout.

and "planted" in puddles of Bonding Agent (Reference Card 12). Some forms of barley grass have a similar tip. The best type is one that used to be sold by the now-defunct firm called Tom Thumb Trees. This is the weed shown in Figure 5–8, although there is little difference between Tom Thumb-style barley grass and any foxtail except that the typical foxtail is shorter and has fewer hairs. The weed in Figure 5–8 has one important advantage that makes it worth searching for. When you have plucked all those individual hairs and planted them, the core of the plant produces a perfect HO- to O-scale model of a tall, leafy weed (Fig. 5–9). One of the only sources of "Tom Thumb" barley grass is along the coastal ranges of California. Foxtails, however, grow just about everywhere, and they lack only that textured core; the hairs are still perfectly suitable weeds for scenes like Figure 5–8.

Cattails, another common weed, can serve the same purpose as foxtails. The hotdog-shaped brown seed pods that form in the fall contain enough hairlike fibers to cover a scale city block (Fig. 5–10). Break off one end of the cattail and pick up the clumps of hairs with

Fig. 5–9 Ed Patrone used a barley grass center stalk for the tall weed near the truck door.

Fig. 5–10 The hairs inside a cattail seed pod are perfect for scale-model weeds. Here they are planted on the edge of an epoxy pond just before the epoxy hardens.

tweezers to "plant" them in puddles of Bonding Agent. The texture and length of the cattail fibers is finer than those from the foxtails, so the two make interesting variations. Both are light beige/brown, but the cattails are a bit lighter. If you want to color these scale-size "weeds" a shade of green, do so after planting the fibers with the Bonding Agent and allowing it to dry for a day or two. Apply the paint with an airbrush, using the colors from Reference Card 16 and the airbrush mixing formula from Reference Card 8 in Chapter 4.

Tumbleweed, Thickets, and Heath

The tight jumble of medium-size twigs that is typical of tumbleweed and such dense undergrowth as thickets and British heather can be simulated with nearly scale-size materials. One material is felt, sold by sewing shops in a variety of colors, including a gray/brown and gray that is similar to the twig colors of many full-size plants. Use a metal-bristle brush such as a file-cleaning "card" (Fig. 5–11) or a steel-wire brush to brush the individual fibers from the surface of the felt. You'll have to comb and pluck the fibers from the bristles. The clumps of fibers can be loosely formed into balls (tumbleweeds) or collected

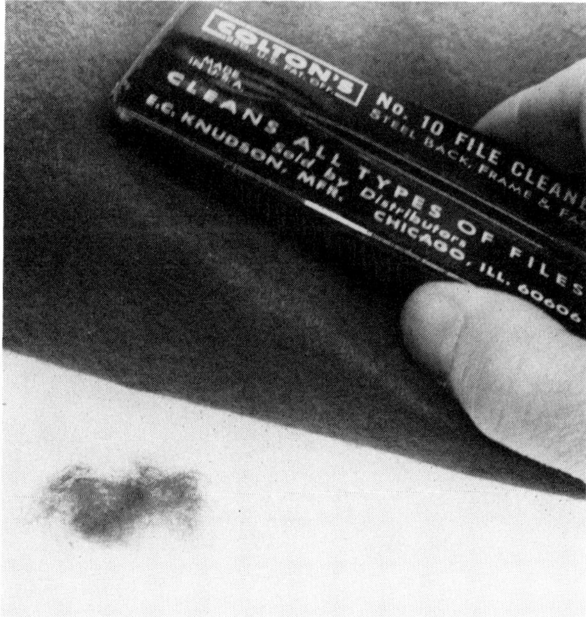

Fig. 5–11 Small tumbleweeds and thick grasses such as heath can be simulated with wool fluff combed from felt with a wire brush.

into large, flat piles to simulate scale-size patches of thickets, such as the southern kudzu weed or British heath. The clumps of felt fiber should be sprayed with Bonding Agent or with a spray adhesive. Sprinkle fine-grind foam over the "twigs" to simulate leaves.

Vines

The availability of fine-grind foam makes the construction of vines simple: Run a bead of artist's matte medium into wiggly lines and sprinkle on some fine-grind foam. The clump of foliage at the base of the vine can be simulated with small pieces of fine cross-section lichen, then sprinkle with fine-grind foam. If you want to duplicate freestanding vines that drape from an overhanging rock or from the trellis in a garden, dip a toothpick in water-base contact cement and lift it out to produce strings of glue. You may have to put some contact cement in a paper cup to let it thicken for a few minutes before it will produce

Fig. 5–12 Noch-brand flocked paper grass can be buried at the edges in fine-grind foam.

Fig. 5–13 The stand-up effect of the Noch grass paper can be duplicated by applying the flocking with Noch's electrostatic dispenser.

the proper length of "string." Drape these strings where you want the vines and *immediately*, before the cement can dry further, sprinkle on some fine ground foam in an appropriate shade of green.

Scale-Size Grass

The European brands of flocking made by the firms of Noch and Sommerfeldt are just about the closest thing yet to scale-size grass (for 1/48 through about 1/24 scale) or weeds (for about 1/87 through 1/48 scale). You can cut your own fibers from polypropylene twine (another macramé product) if you want a slightly longer or shorter fiber. Noch and Sommerfeldt offer their flocking as "grass mats" (Fig. 5–12), and nearly every fiber stands straight up like real grass. These mats can be ripped into ragged-edge patches and buried in a mixture of Bonding Agent, Soaking Agent, and ground foam as shown in Figure 5–12. Preiser offers similar flocking on plastic backings that simulate marshes, swamps, and ponds. Noch and Sommerfeldt also offer loose flocking in plastic bags. Noch even has an electrostatic applicator that allows you to apply the flocking with a spraying action by simply squeezing the plastic applicator bottle (Fig. 5–13). An electrostatic charge makes the individual strands stick straight up when they hit puddles of artist's matte medium. (Use the medium straight from the bottle because it dries with a flat, nongloss finish.) Only 60 or 70 percent of the fibers will stand straight up, and not as many on the Noch or Sommerfeldt flocked paper. For incredible realism, add a few clumps of the foxtail or cattail fibers here and there, then air brush the area with Polly S paints.

Chapter 6

Trees: From Aspen to Weeping Willow

Realistic trees can be made in only two ways. They can be built by hand from scenery components, or ready-made trees can be modified and repainted. Considering the hundreds of different ready-made trees made by firms like Bachmann and Life-Like, there would seem to be a limitless variety to choose from. Not so. The best ready-builts have an unnaturally bright green that is too evenly distributed, and there are usually gaps where the branches attach to the trunk. But almost all ready-made trees, including those kits of plastic discs shaped like pine boughs and those faintly disguised bottle brushes, are candidates for realistic trees. There are also several hundred different tree *kits*, and nearly all of them are well worthwhile if you take the time to modify them. There are also some suitable custom-made trees from firms like AMSI and Chama Timber Company.

Ready-Made Trees

A considerable amount of labor is required to produce even the simplest tree miniature. Ready-made trees are manufactured as inexpensively as possible, and there are basically only two types. One is literally a twisted wire core with plastic bristles, just like a bottle-cleaning brush, covered with ground foam. The length of the bristles and the shape and color of the ground foam determine whether it is a "pine" or an "oak." The second type has a molded plastic trunk and branch structure (much like AHM, Kibri, and Bachmann tree *kits*) with large clumps of colored lichen moss glued in place. Both types of trees can be converted into realistic models with a good deal of

Fig. 6–1 Ed Patrone used small branches from mesquite, sagebrush, and scrub oak to make the tree trunks for this forest.

work, but they are not the ideal that you should be striving for when you make your own.

Bottle-Brush Trees

Bottle-brush trees (Fig. 6–16) can be effective for simulating a complete coniferous forest that might cover a square yard or two of mountainside on a model railroad. The trees are available in heights ranging from about two inches to nearly a foot, so you can place the larger trees around the edges of your forest and gradually decrease the size of the trees toward the center and toward the tops of mountains to create a "forced perspective" that will make the forest look even larger than it is (see Chapter 9). There are three steps involved in increasing the realism of bottle-brush trees: (1) bend the wire trunks into slight S bends to simulate the effect of a real trunk; (2) use a pair of heavy scissors to trim the ends of the bristles in a more random pattern, trimming some of the bristles right down to their base in the twisted wire trunk; and (3) paint any visible portions of the trunk, including areas where you've trimmed the bristles close to the trunk, and spray the "needles" with at least two shades of green to give highlights and contrasts (see Reference Cards 16 and 19).

Lichen-Moss Trees

Lichen-moss and plastic-trunked trees can be improved with a similar three-step process: (1) paint the trunks in appropriate shades of brown and gray; (2) dab some full-strength artist's matte medium randomly around the plastic limbs and the lichen, then sprinkle on some medium-grind foam to vary the too-rounded shape of the lichen; and (3) spray the lichen portion of the tree with 3M "Sprayment" (work in a well-ventilated area) or dip the tops of the lichen, using the tree trunk as your handle, into Bonding Agent (see Reference Card 12), then sprinkle on fine-grind foam. The lichen trees will always be too thick because of the dense understructure of the lichen that represents the twigs. However, these trees can make nice background details, or they can be used to form the inner portion of a forest where the outer trees made from kits or scratch-built with a finer, see-through twig and leaf technique.

Building Trees from Kits

Model railroad shops carry a dozen different brands of tree kits and nearly 100 varieties of conifers, deciduous trees, and palms. Purchase Walthers' *HO Railroad Catalog* and Volume 4 of JMC International's *Source Book*, which contains scenery, tools, and electrical supplies, to get an idea of the incredible array of tree kits that are available. The tree kits from Walthers, Campbell, and Color-Rite include all components plus instructions in a single box. You should build at least one of every type of tree kit you can buy at your local shop or through mail order to give you self-confidence and the opportunity to try different techniques. You can then buy bulk materials of the brand and

Tree Trunk, Stump, and Log Colors

Color	Use	Artist's Acrylics	Polly S Paint	Glidden Interior Latex Paint
Gray-brown	Tree bark	Van Dyke	Roof Brown PR70 or Dark Earth Brown PF64	1 part Hickory 1 part Night Owl
Red-brown	Tree bark	Burnt Sienna	Boxcar Red PR74	Wild Turkey
Gray-white	Tree bark	9 parts White 1 part Burnt Sienna	Dust PR3	1 part Cobweb 1 part Night Owl
Shading	All tree bark colors	3 parts Lamp Black 1 part White	Grimy Black PF14	Night Owl
Highlights	All tree bark colors	19 parts White 1 part Burnt Sienna	Antique PF16	Chalk

Note: Apply with dry-brush technique, or as a wash thinned with 9 parts water or denatured alcohol to 1 part mixed paint.

Exposed Wood				
Fresh cuts	Stumps and log ends	8 parts White 1 part Burnt Sienna 1 part Yellow Ochre	2 parts Antique PF16 1 part Mud PR83	2 parts Chalk 1 part Ponce de Leon
Old cuts	Stumps and log ends	17 parts White 1 part Burnt Sienna 1 part Yellow Ochre 1 part Lamp Black	7 parts Antique PF16 1 part Grimy Black PF14 2 parts Mud PR83	7 parts Chalk 1 part Night Owl 2 parts Ponce de Leon

Note: Apply the shading and highlights for bark to stumps and log ends for a similar effect.

combine commercial materials with natural or handmade trunks using the patterns in Figures 6–18 to 6–31.

Woodland Scenics' Tree Kits

Woodland Scenics has done more than any other firm to bring easy-to-build, realistic trees into general distribution. The kits contain traditional cast-metal tree trunks. The cast-metal trunk and large branch structures are flexible enough to be bent into a variety of shapes, then painted. Woodland Scenics also makes a special "Foliage Material," which is made of brown/gray fibers or hairs (much like macramé fiber) with fine-grind polyurethane foam glued to the fibers. This material makes creating realistic twigs and leaves virtually foolproof. The only trick in using it is to pull it apart and stretch it as thinly as possible so that the finished tree has a "see-*through*" look. An average pad of "Foliage Material," about 4 × 4 inches, should be stretched to about 12 × 12 inches to give the appearance shown in Figure 6–2. Work

Fig. 6–2 Woodland Scenics' "Foliage Material" should look like this after you have stretched it to its limit.

Fig. 6–3 The amount of "Foliage Material" used on Woodland Scenics' "Columnar Pine" trees shows how easy it is to alter the texture of a kit-built tree. These trees are similar in shape to the black spruce. Photo courtesy Woodland Scenics.

over a newspaper and save the foam that falls off for other scenic textures. You will find that at least a half-cup of loose foam remains after you have stretched the material, and that's the way it's supposed to be. With scissors, cut it into small blocks for a deciduous tree or into triangles for a conifer. Dab some undiluted artist's matte medium onto the branches and stick the material in place. Work from the bottom of the trunk upward. Trim any loose strands with scissors.

Work Stands for Simplified Tree Building

Woodland Scenics' tree kits and some other brands include a pin that protrudes downward from the base of the tree trunk. The pin supports the tree when you plant it in the plaster scenery by drilling a similar-size hole in the plaster. You will need such a pin or nail in any tree. If the kit does not include the pin, or if you are making your own trees, drill a hole in the base of the tree and glue a nail into the hole. The pin is also used to support the tree while you apply the twig and foliage materials. Drill a slightly larger hole in a scrap of wood to hold the pin (Figure 6–4).

AMSI, Bachmann, AHM, and Kibri Tree Kits

AMSI, Bachmann, AHM, and Kibri kits are finished with a leaf texture of finely ground polyurethane foam, but the materials for the trunks and twig structure are different. AMSI, like Woodland Scenics, uses a cast-metal tree trunk structure, but some of the AMSI trunks are painted and the smaller limbs are easier to bend. AMSI tree trunks are available as separate pieces in a variety of sizes, while Woodland Scenics trunks are sold only as part of a complete kit. Because the AHM, Bachmann and Kibri trunks are plastic, they are not as realistic as the AMSI or Woodland Scenics trunks, but they are much cheaper. The plastic trunks must be heated with a flame from a match or cigarette lighter to soften the plastic so that the branches can be bent.

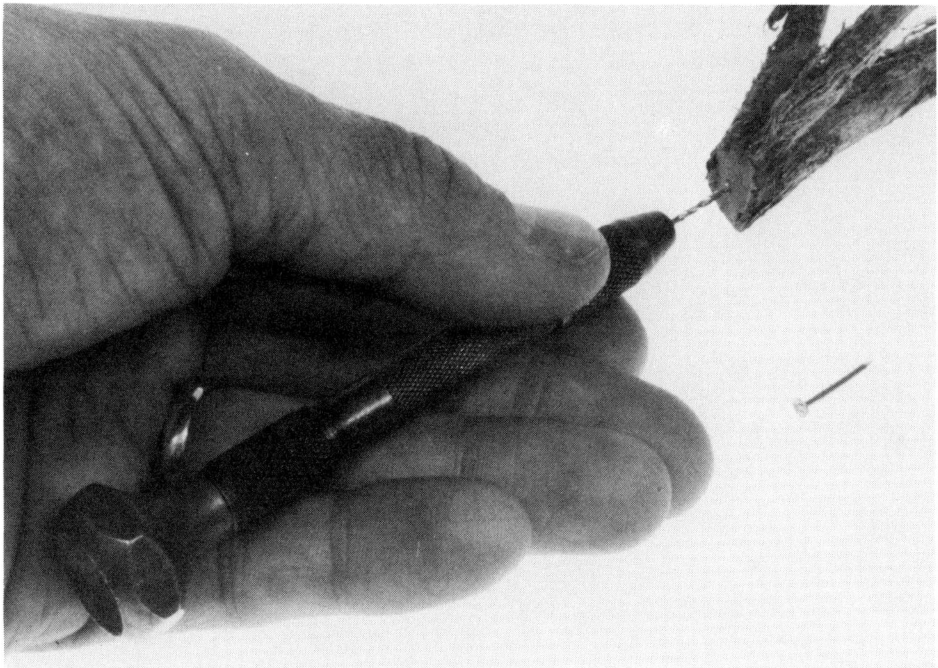

Fig. 6–4 Use a pin vise to hold the drill bit while drilling a hole in the base of the tree trunk for a supporting nail (right).

This is a tricky process that demands just enough flame to soften the plastic but not enough to melt it. Too hot a flame can also ignite the plastic itself, so keep a bucket of water handy to drop the tree into and wear gloves and goggles.

AMSI is the only firm that uses steel wool, prepainted brown, for the intermediate branches. AHM, Bachmann, and Kibri use a synthetic fiber similar to macramé fibre for the twig structure. The fiber must be pulled apart to produce a more open "mesh," cut into chunks with scissors, then cemented to the trunk and limb structures with artist's matte medium. Do not use white glue; it leaves a shine, whereas matte medium dries with a flat finish. The fiber mesh can be sprayed with glue (like 3M "Sprayment") or dipped into Bonding Agent (Reference

Fig. 6–5 Fine steel wire (about 30 gauge) was covered with shreds of steel wool and fine-grind foam by AMSI's professionals to make this 1/24 scale weeping willow tree.

Card 12) and sprinkled with fine-grind foam. The steel wool or fiber mesh allows considerable versatility in shaping the tree. The illustrations of typical tree shapes in Figures 6–18 to 6–31 show the trunk and limb structure as a darker shape than the twig and leaf portion of each tree. The twig and leaf portion must be shaped with the steel wool or fiber. The ground foam adds only texture, not shape, to kit-built or handmade trees.

Scenic Craft and Other All-Plastic Trees

Molded plastic trees, which are inexpensive and quick to build, are good for areas where several dozen or even several hundred trees are needed. The most common tree kits are the conifers from Bachmann (Plasticville), Faller, and Kibri. The Kibri trees are stacked discs of plastic that simulate tree boughs. An entire chapter in Volume 3 of *The Model Railroading Handbook* is devoted to these and Scenic Craft's trees. Scenic Craft's "Pine Trees" and "Shade Trees" (Fig. 6–6) are available in two sizes as one-piece flexible plastic moldings.

Other sources of plastic trees include small pine trees sold by some craft supply stores, pieces of plastic Christmas trees or wreaths, and plastic "seaweed" sold by pet shops for aquariums (Fig. 6–6). These trees can be treated and textured in the same way as the others. All of them have far too many branches, so you must cut one-quarter to as much as three-quarters of the branches from the trunk with scissors. Next, bend the branches at random angles. Scenic Craft's "Shade Trees," in fact, can be converted into pine trees by bending all of the remaining branches downward. Spray the trunks and limbs with gray-brown paint, spray the trees with either 3M "Sprayment" or dip them in Bonding Agent, and sprinkle on fine-grind foam. The Bachmann, Faller, and Kibri pine trees made from stacked discs of "boughs" should be treated with fine-grind foam in the same manner.

Campbell and Color-Rite Tree Kits

Campbell and Color-Rite tree kits use a natural growth similar to air fern to simulate the branches and needles on conifers. The Campbell kit uses a preshaped and colored wooden trunk, while the Color-Rite trunks are molded. To assemble either brand, cut the natural growth to length and insert the pieces into predrilled holes in the trunks. Drill a hole in the base of the trunks and insert a nail (see Fig. 6–4) to support the trees while assembling and planting them. The

Fig. 6–6 Inexpensive plastic trees; Scenic Craft's "Pine Trees" (upper left) and "Shade Trees" (upper right), a craft store pine (lower left), two pieces of plastic Christmas trees (center bottom), and plastic seaweed (lower right).

bright green air fern should be modified by spraying on a wash of gray-green or greenish-yellow (see Reference Card 16). The resulting tree shapes are most similar to white pines (Fig. 6–29), but they can be altered to match other species by drilling more holes for more air fern and/or by substituting asparagus fern (Fig. 6–8) or "Foliage Material." The flowered portions of caspia weeds can be treated with fine-grind foam and inserted in holes in the trunks to match a real tree with thick, upswept boughs, such as the red pine in Figure 6–28.

Fig. 6–7 Albert Hetzel assembled this Color-Rite pine tree kit. It resembles the white pine in its shape.

Using Natural Growths for Trees

Three general categories of weeds, ferns, twigs, and other natural growths are suitable for miniature trees: (1) growths that simulate only the branch structure, (2) growths that simulate the trunk and major branch structure, and (3) growths that simulate the needles and small limbs of conifers. Figure 6–8 shows the most common growths. The materials used in Figure 6–9 are suitable for a variety of tree trunk and limbs. Figure 6–10 shows the unusual Pride of Madera plant in its dormant state with small triangles of "Foliage Material" simulating the boughs of a conifer. Dick Harley and Dave Hussey developed the technique of using the Pride of Madera by trimming its curled ends and gluing on triangles of "Foliage Material" with Bonding Agent.

It is never wise to use natural growth to simulate the leaves of deciduous trees in any model built to a scale smaller than about 1/40.

Fig. 6–8 Natural growths are often available at craft supply stores, if you cannot locate them on fall field trips. Left to right: yarrow, caspia, air fern (top), asparagus fern (middle), four pine cones, and spirea.

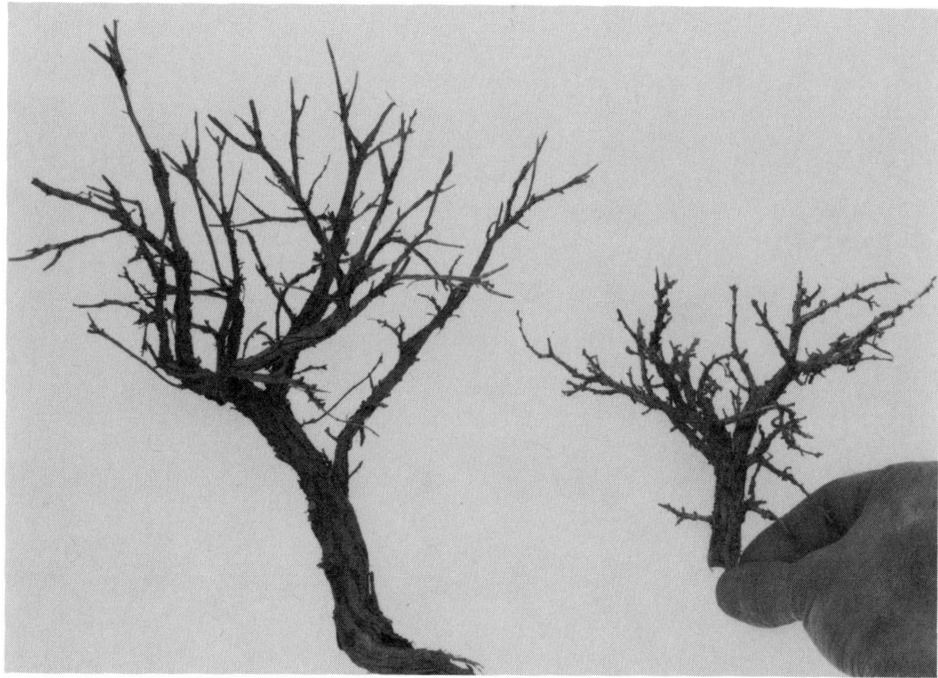

Fig. 6–9 Walthers includes real mesquite trunks (right) in the "Gnarled Oak" tree kits. Dead sagebrush (left) also works well for trunks.

Natural growth is often fine enough, but the textures do not look like scale-model *leaves*. For 1/40 scale or larger, caspia weed can be glued together and a trunk shaped with water putty, a fine plasterlike substance sold by hardware stores. Charles Bowdish and Herman Mike used this technique in Figure 6–11 for the Buhl Planetarium's diorama in Pittsburgh. For larger trees, the Buhl Planetarium makes trunks and limbs from wire (Fig. 6–12) with water-putty "bark" and limbs and leaves from the tips of caspia or yarrow. These same tree-building techniques can be used for trees in smaller scales by shaking or cutting the dried flowers from the ends of the weeds. The fine branch structures can then be grouped into trunks, held with white glue, and the trunks textured with water putty. After the trunk is painted, the twig structure of either macramé fiber or "Foliage Material" and "leaves" of fine-grind foam can be added. Lonnie Shay uses hand-carved balsa wood trunks with caspia weed "boughs" glued into holes that he presses

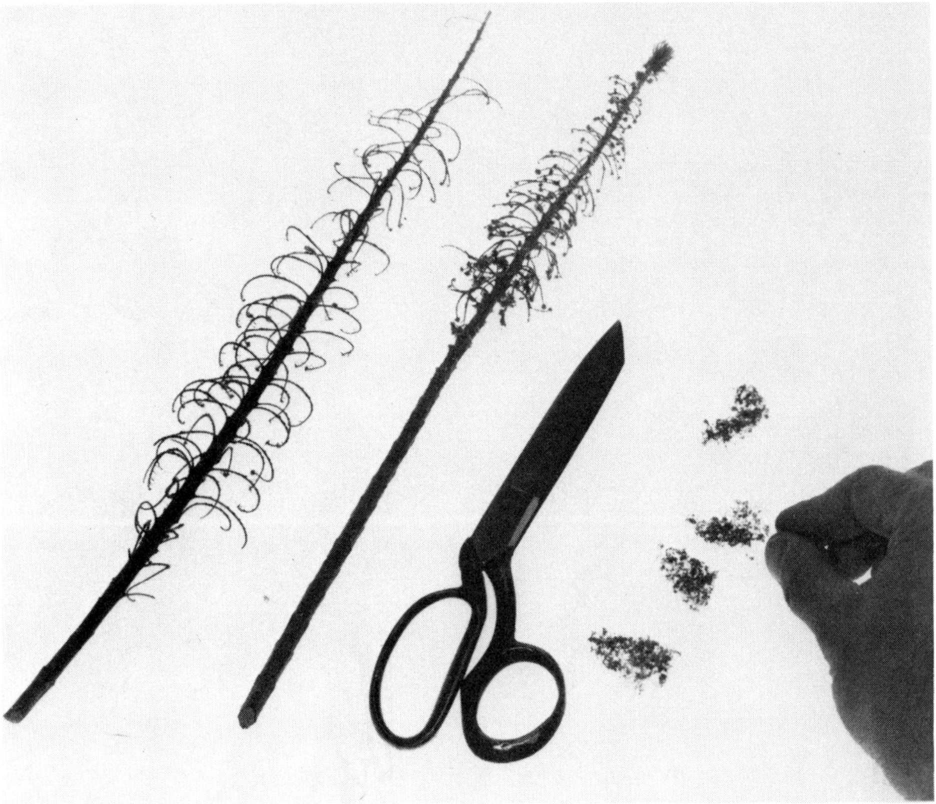

Fig. 6–10 Pride of Madera plants (left) make excellent trunk and branch structures for pine trees when covered with small triangles of Woodland Scenics' "Foliage Material" (right).

into the soft balsa with a knitting needle (Fig. 6–13); the coniferous needles are simulated with medium-grind foams. Caspia and yarrow are usually sold by craft supply or florists shops if you cannot locate them in the wild. The Pride of Madera grows along the coastal mountains of California.

Some types of pine cones can simulate small pine tree models of about 2 to 4 inches in height. The cones must have been lying on the ground long enough for birds and animals to have eaten the seeds, leaving only the hairlike inner core (Figs. 6–8 and 6–14). The cones need not be painted, but they must be covered with a light texture of

Fig. 6–11 Caspia weeds can be used as texture and the branch structure if several are grouped into each tree. The shapes of these trees are similar to American elms.

fine-grind foam. Spray the foam and just the tips of the branches with an appropriate shade of green.

Do-It-Yourself Tree-Building

Certainly, every tree assembled from a kit or from natural growths, ground polyurethane foam, or Woodland Scenics' "Foliage Material" is a do-it-yourself project. Some modelers, though, have created some clever and effective alternatives to tree construction. Jack Rice uses simple wooden meat skewers with clumps of "Foliage Material" and leftover foam to make conifers (Fig. 6–14). The skewers are painted a bark color and when the paint dries, they are dipped in undiluted

Fig. 6–12 The trunk and branch structure for this tree was made from several pieces of 10-gauge electrical wire covered with water putty and paint. The shape is similar to the oak.

artist's matte medium. Round clumps of stretched "Foliage Material" are pushed over the skewer and some loose ground foam sprinkled on before the matte medium dries.

Charles Bowdish uses $\frac{1}{4}$- to 2-inch lengths of sisal rope, cut with scissors and unraveled into individual strands, to make the "bristles" or "boughs" on his bottle-brush trees (Fig. 6–16). The trunk is steel wire, about 20 gauge, twisted into a rope with a hand drill. He clamps two strands of the wire in a vise, lays the boughs over the two wires, and twists the whole thing together. It's similar to the technique used to make the ready-made pine trees sold by AHM, Bachmann, Faller, Life-Like, and Noch, except that the sisal produces a more random

Fig. 6–13 Lonnie Shay carves balsa wood trunks and uses caspia (right) for the branches and ground foam for texture. These trees are similar to red pines.

Fig. 6–14 Jack Rice painted pine cones gray/brown and textured them with fine-grind foam to simulate small firs on his HO-scale layout. Shape is similar to the balsam fir.

appearance. The boughs are then painted green and fine-grind foam sprinkled on for texture, like the custom-made trees from Chama Timber Company.

Tree Trunk Construction

There is no suitable substitute for the dried roots of weeds (Fig. 11–4), a real hedge clipping (Fig. 11–1), sagebrush, or mesquite to simulate the trunk of a tree. These growths, however, can be used only to simulate certain species of tree. AMSI or Woodland Scenics cast-metal trunks can be used for most kinds of trees, but both brands have a limited selection of shapes of more than about 4 inches in height.

Fig. 6–15 For nearly instant trees, Jack Rice uses Woodland Scenics' "Foliage Material" from the box with matching fine-grind foam to texture wooden meat skewers. The shapes are similar to the Douglas firs.

For larger trees or unusual shapes, or simply to save money you will want to make some trunks for yourself. Figure 6–17 shows the four steps for building the root system, tree trunk, and branches for just about any size tree. Stranded clothesline cable or 10-gauge insulated electrical wire will produce a tree in the 4- to 8-inch range, depending on how rounded or oblong the shape. For larger trees, twist two or more pieces of wire or cable together in the main trunk area. This method allows you to model the often-visible upper roots of a tree. The root system also gives the tree extra support, and the taproot provides the peg for holding the tree while modeling it and planting it.

Fig. 6–16 Charles Bowdish and other modelers at the Buhl Planetarium use unraveled sisal rope fibers and fine steel wire to wind their own bottle-brush trees. Some fine-grind foam would improve the appearance. The shape is similar to the balsam fir.

Tree Patterns for Modelers

The fourteen patterns in Figures 6–18 to 6–31 allow you to match most tree kits to the shape and texture of nearly any tree. The species shown are only one example of the type of tree that has that shape and texture. Remember that the health and age of a tree can alter its appearance (Figs. 6–32 and 6–33), so vary the shapes of all your trees. Use the darker lines in Figure 6-17 to shape cast-metal or wire trunks and limbs. The lighter-shaded areas must be shaped with macramé fibers, the similar material in AHM and Bachmann kits, or the mesh and foam "Foliage Material" from Woodland Scenics. The texture of the tree is achieved with either medium-grind for some conifers with "clumps" of needles or fine-grind foam. For variety, paper punchings that are left over when some banks cancel checks or the punchings

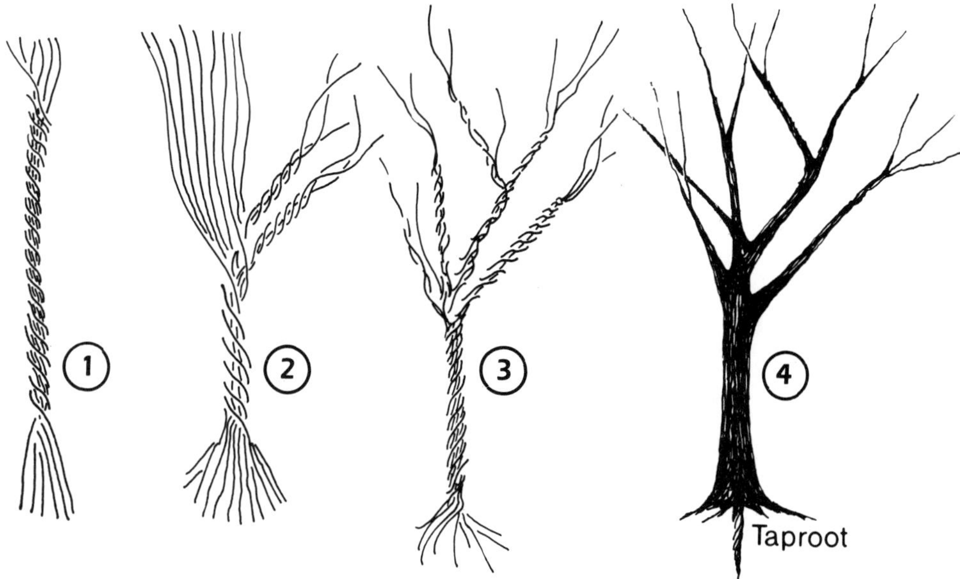

Step 1: Cut 10-gauge electrical wire (insulation not shown) or stranded wire clothesline cable.

Step 2: Unravel portions of the upper ends for branches and twigs. Unravel the lower ends for root.

Step 3: Twist the individual strands of twig wires into branches.

Step 4: Texture the exposed root system, trunk, and branches with water putty.

Fig. 6–17 The four steps in creating a root system, tree trunk, limb structure from 10-gauge electrical wire or stranded clothesline cable.

from some Telex machines can be dyed to simulate leaves and used as texture.

Palm Trees

The modeler has two choices if he needs palm trees for a diorama or model railroad. Buy a Preiser kit (Fig. 6–34), or build one using the techniques Willard Jones applied to his HO-scale palms (Fig. 6–35). The Preiser kits are fine if the species and size (about 9 inches) of the model is suitable. To duplicate Willard Jones's balsa wood palms, scrape a wood saw blade along the soft balsa. For rough, scalelike palm bark, wrap Campbell's HO-scale paper roof shingles around the

Fig. 6–18 Black cherry.

Fig. 6–19 White oak.

142

Fig. 6–21 Gray birch.

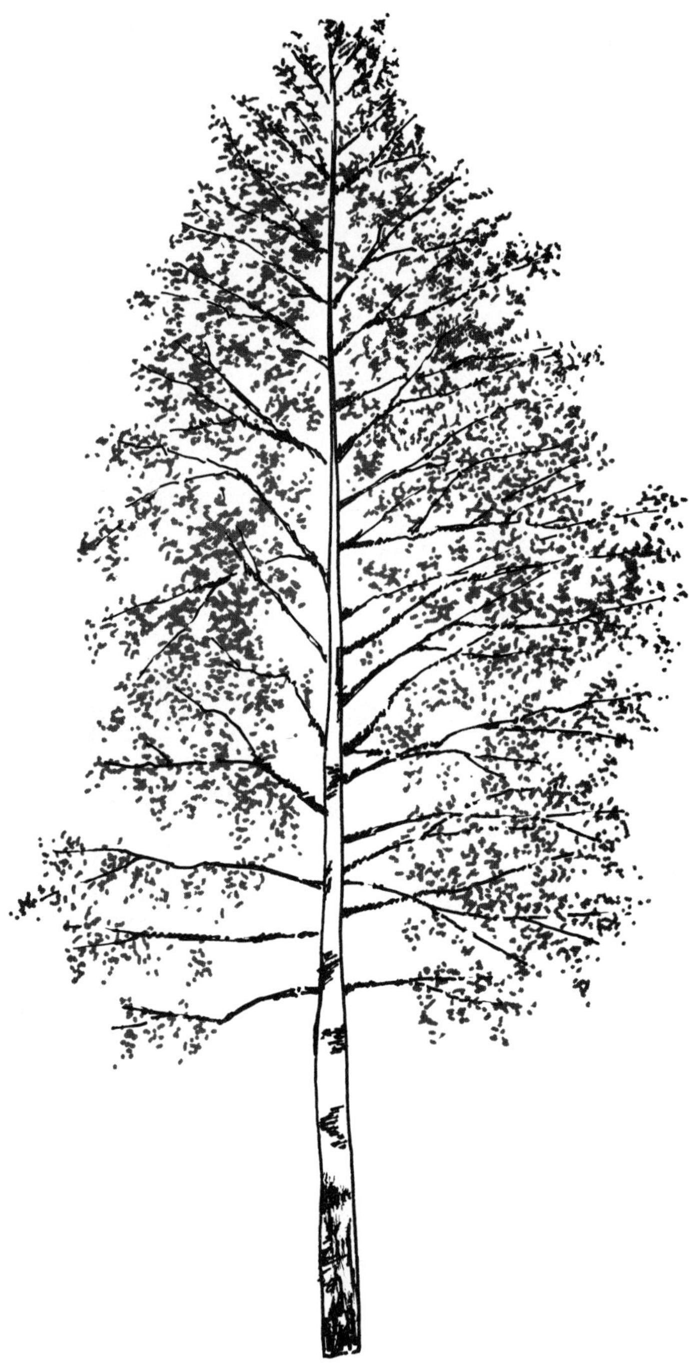

Fig. 6–22 Quaking aspen.

Fig. 6–23 Weeping willow.

145

Fig. 6–24 Lombardy poplar.

Fig. 6–25 Balsam fir.

Fig. 6–26 Mature Douglas fir.

Fig. 6–27 Young Douglas fir.

Fig. 6–28 Red pine.

Fig. 6–29 White pine.

Fig. 6–30 White spruce.

Fig. 6–31 Black spruce.

153

Fig. 6–32 A typical conifer during the basic stages of its life cycle.

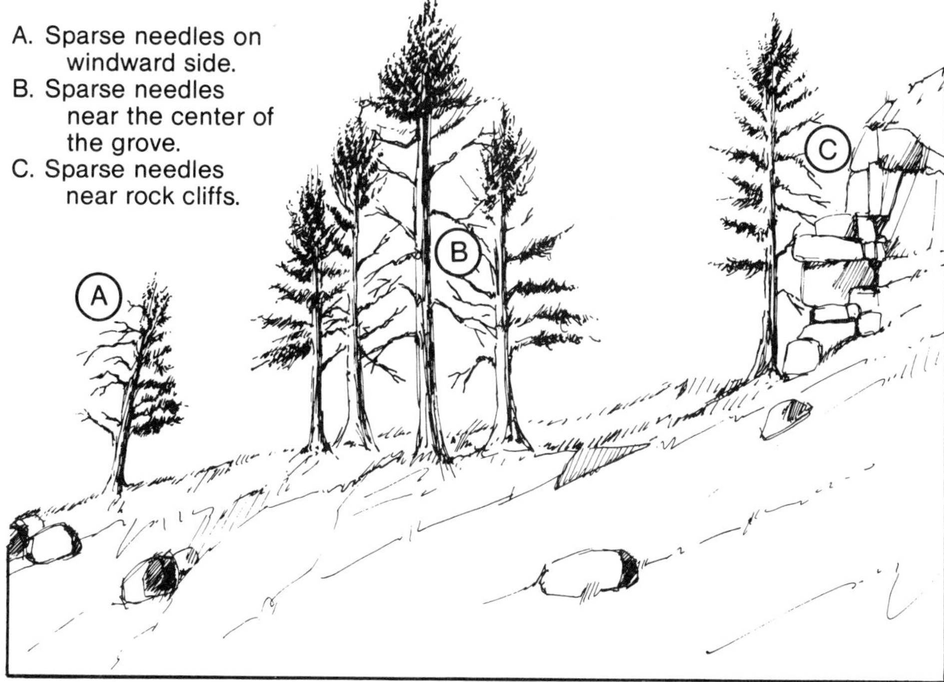

Fig. 6–33 The effect of weather and adjacent cliffs on the foliage of conifers. The effect on deciduous trees is similar.

tree. The dead palm fronds and seeds can be simulated with white wool or synthetic macramé twine dyed the proper color (see Reference Card 17). Unravel it and glue it to the trunk with artist's matte medium. The actual palm fronds are green-colored feathers, available at craft supply stores for making imitation flowers. Weather the fronds with some beige to tone down their bright green hues (see Reference Card 16).

Planting Trees

No miniature tree is complete until it is planted in the diorama. Figure 6–33 shows how the site for each tree can affect its growth. Of course, you must make adjustments in the "normal" pattern of twigs, leaves, or needles when you build the trees for special locations. Trees

Fig. 6–34 Preiser palm tree kits are all plastic. The completed tree is shown at left.

do not always grow straight out of the ground, but the effect of nearly any leaning tree is not realistic in a miniature scene. Except for some dead or dying trees, *all* model trees must be positioned to stand straight. The pin that protrudes from the bottom of the trunk will secure the tree, but you may have to mix a small batch of molding plaster, plaster of paris, or even water putty with some color to pack around the base of the trunk. The plaster will hold the tree upright, and you can shape and carve it to simulate exposed roots. If you don't want to bother with modeling roots, cover the base of the tree with dirt or brown ground foam and hold it in place with Bonding Agent. Grass seldom

Fig. 6–35 Willard Jones made these towering palms using balsa trunks, twine leaf shards, and feathers.

grows around the roots of trees, but you may want to use some yellow-gray ground foam or paper punchings to simulate fallen leaves. Don't forget, as most modelers do, that nearly all stands of mature trees are surrounded by a few fresh saplings. And remember that it is rare for a single tree to grow in the wild; trees usually grow in small groves of at least three.

Forests

Few modelers attempt to duplicate dense forests, but the technique is nearly as quick as covering the same surface area with any other texture. For a dense forest, model two or three rows of "complete"

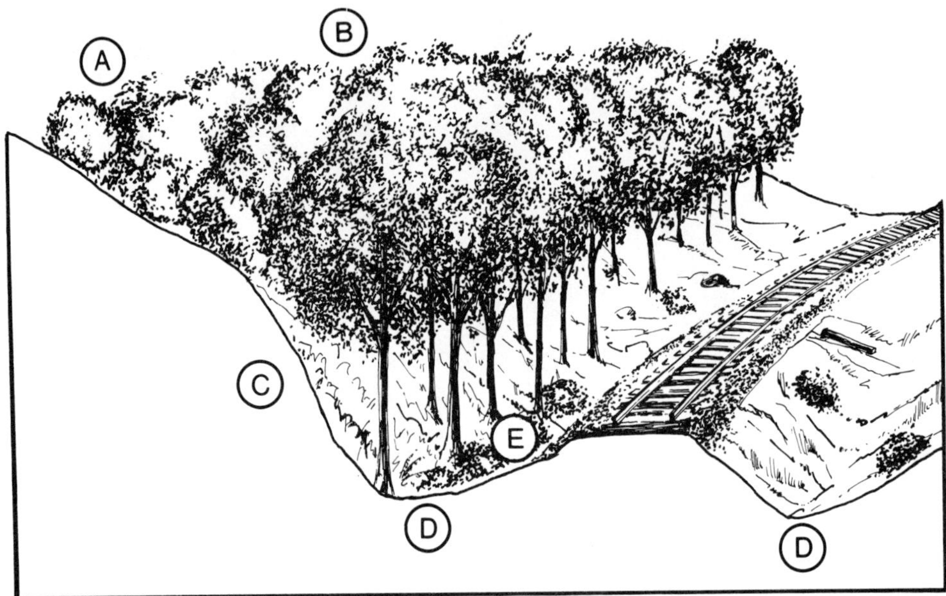

A. Smaller treetops of finer texture.
B. Treetops of similar size and texture; these imply "whole" trees, even where no trunks exist.
C. Slope angles uphill to disguise the lack of trunks on the back rows of trees.
D. Drainage ditches.
E. Undergrowth.

Fig. 6–36 A cutaway view showing how a dense forest can be simulated with just a few completed trees on the edges. Twig and foliage textures without trunks make up the rest of the forest.

trees and trunks along the outer edges of the forest (Fig. 6–36). Bring the plaster hillside upward behind these first rows of trees and plant the upper halves of all remaining trees. Before planting the inner groves, paint the plaster dark brown to simulate the floor of a shaded forest. Obviously, this technique demands some preplanning in the shape of the plaster scenery. If you use the Hydrocal and paper-towel technique for hillsides that is described in Chapter 4, you can build up the hillside with wadded-up newspapers and cover them with the Hydrocal-soaked paper towels. You might also want to include a rock casting or two (see Chapter 4) to simulate exposed boulders or cliffs above the tops of the trees.

Chapter 7

Water and Seascapes

There is no more visually exciting miniature scenic effect than water. "State of the art" has a double meaning when applied to the simulation of water in miniature. Two nearly odor-free products, epoxy and artist's gloss medium, produce crystal clear, sturdy surfaces that look so much like water you have to touch them to believe they are not real. The pioneer model makers' search for ways to make real water practical have at last been rewarded with materials that, for the modeler, truly are *better* than water.

Beginning at the Bottom

Epoxy and artist's gloss medium have one thing in common with real water. They run like water while they are still fluid. This means that they will spread perfectly level. Both will flow through even a pinhole-size gap in the plaster scenery, but the problems of self-leveling and leaking will not be critical on small streams or rapids where the simulated water is brushed on. Small ponds, wide streams, lakes, or harbors *must* be prepared for the epoxy or gloss medium by completely sealing the plaste surface. Perhaps the best sealer is full-strength latex interior wall paint in an appropriate earth shade with enough white or toner mixed in to match the surrounding soil or dirt. Never sift any loose foam, real dirt, or any other loose texture onto the bottom of any watercourse. Air bubbles become trapped and are visible, particularly when epoxy cures and hardens. The air bubbles look like submerged diamonds, and they permanently destroy the realism of the scene. The problem is not quite so acute with artist's gloss medium,

Fig. 7–1 Partially submerged logs are enclosed in the last three or four $\frac{1}{8}$-inch-thick pours of epoxy to make a simulated logging pond.

but it is not effective for model water that is more than about $\frac{1}{4}$ inch or so deep. Mask off the stream area while you texture the surrounding surfaces and, to be safe, vacuum the bottom of any watercourse just before you pour in the epoxy or gloss medium.

Streams and Ponds

Just about any shiny or clear glossy paint could be used to simulate small streams and ponds. But most of these paints have an offensive odor and are difficult to clean up. Artist's gloss medium dries glossy and almost clear. Because it has a water base, it is less likely to discolor

Simulated Water

Type of Water	Body of Water	Material
Deep water	Rivers Lakes Harbors	Two-part epoxy resins, such as Envirotex or Ultra-Glo. The epoxies usually require an equal mixture of resin and hardener. (Casting resins require a few drops of hardener or catalyst and produce more heat and odor while curing.) Dyes such as those sold by CHEMCO for casting resins can also be used in most epoxy resins to provide a slight blue or blue-green cast.
Shallow water	Streams Ponds	Artist's gloss medium, a clear acrylic-type paint that can be applied thick enough to form ripples. It dries to a high-gloss finish with little odor.
Rapid water	Rapids Waterfalls Simulated waves in harbors	Form basic wave shapes with plaster for deep rapids and harbor scenes. For shallow rapids, form the bottom of the stream with plaster rocks. For waterfalls, use surgical glass wool, available from wholesale medical supply firms, stringing the wool for the vertical waterfall and crumpling it into balls for the foam effect at the base. Coat the wool with several applications of gloss medium, touching the final crests with dabs of pearl-white fingernail polish. Wear rubber gloves when working with the wool.

Colors for Epoxy Water

Color	Use	Formula
Blue-green	Mountain streams Rivers	1 drop blue resin dye 1 drop green resin dye 4 ounces epoxy Mix thoroughly while blending resin and hardener.
Blue	Deep lakes Harbors	12 drops blue resin dye 4 ounces epoxy Mix thoroughly while blending resin and hardener.
Gray-green	Harbors Oceans Deep rivers Lakes and ponds	1 drop green resin dye 1 drop black resin dye 8 ounces epoxy Mix thoroughly while blending resin and hardener.
Brown	Flooded rivers Shallow streams Ponds	1 drop resin dye 4 ounces epoxy Mix thoroughly while blending resin and hardener.
White	Crest of waves Waterfalls Rapids Breakers	1 part white acrylic 2 parts gloss medium Paint and allow to dry thoroughly. Apply small dabs of pearl-white fingernail polish to crests of waves and foam.
Clear final coat	"Wet" look	Apply at least $\frac{1}{32}$ inch of epoxy or a thick layer of gloss medium over the final layer of colored resin. Work small waves into epoxy during the last few minutes of hardening.

R C 21

the bottom of the watercourse. Use a good quality brush or an eye dropper to apply the gloss medium exactly where you want it. The easiest way to simulate ponds is to pour the gloss medium into the depression that will form the pond until the edges of the pond have filled the intended area. You'll achieve a perfectly natural meandering shoreline with this method and be assured that the surface will be level. The gloss medium is thick enough to brush up some small peaks, and they will dry to form natural ripples on the surface. The pouring technique can also be used to create "natural" small streams. However, this method is risky because you may find that the pockets and hollows of the stream become just a series of ponds. Small streams can be simulated far more effectively and with more control by brushing the gloss medium exactly where you *hope* the stream will flow.

Using Decoupage Epoxy for Water

The decoupage craft has been responsible for the creation of several different types of plastic materials that dry crystal clear and with a hard surface. Recently these compounds have been improved so that virtually no undesirable odor is produced as the material cures from its liquid to a solid state. The better known brands are Envirotex and Chemco Ultra-Glo "1:1 Polymer Coating," a special two-part epoxy that has little odor. It differs from the resins recommended in the three volumes of *The Model Railroading Handbook:* that the "hardener" fluid (or catalyst) is mixed in a 1:1 ratio with the resin. The previous materials were mixed with just a few drops of hardener to a cup of resin, and they produce an unpleasant, if not unhealthful, odor. New epoxies seem to have all the advantages of these older resins without the disadvantages. Mix the decoupage hardener and resin thoroughly and in equal parts. You may want to add a drop or two of special resin dye (the type used in casting resins) to the mixture to duplicate special water conditions. Never use a conventional two-part epoxy, which is too thick to provide a level waterlike flow.

There is no particular limit to the surface area you can cover with a single pouring of Envirotex. However, limit the *depth* of each pour to $\frac{1}{8}$ inch or less to avoid cracking. If you mix too much, pour it into another watercourse before it cures. Heat speeds the curing process, so you might want to hold a light bulb near the "water" surface until

Fig. 7–2 Mix Envirotex in old cans or paper cups. A fresh cup should be used for each pour.

it cures (Fig. 7–3). Work in a room that is fairly warm, about 70 degrees or warmer. In a cooler room, keep a light bulb or two burning near the "water." The fluid cures with just the faintest hint of a ripple on the surface, which is too "calm" for any scale-model pond or lake. Poke at the surface with a wooden tongue depressor or ice-cream stick just as the resin begins to cure or set; the pockets will *almost* smooth over to form gentle ripples in the surface. If the lake, river, or harbor is supposed to be more than about 2 inches deep, reduce its depth by pouring precolored molding plaster or plaster of paris into the "valley." Color the plaster to match the surrounding areas, but mix it to the consistency of thick cream so that it will be self-leveling. Stop pouring the plaster when the level is within the 2-inch minimum of what will later be the top surface of the decoupage epoxy water.

Fig. 7–3 A light bulb can be held near the epoxy to speed up curing time and help create gentle ripples in the hardened surface. Do not allow the hot bulb to touch the surface of the "water."

Coloring Envirotex or Ultra-Glo

If you are creating a lake or harbor with $1\frac{1}{2}$ to 2 inches of epoxy, add enough navy blue dye to the mixture to make the plaster lake or harbor bottom virtually invisible after that first $\frac{1}{8}$-inch-thick pouring of epoxy. Add just a trace of the dye to the next few pours and no dye at all to the last pour or two. You will discover that you can simulate very deep water with as little as $\frac{1}{2}$ inch of Envirotex using this dye technique. You can skip that first dark dye by pouring the flat plaster bottom, then spraying the flat surface with navy blue paint. Allow the plaster and paint to dry for at least a week before pouring the epoxy. With this technique, all of the "depth" of the lake or harbor except that last $\frac{1}{2}$ inch is actually plaster. This technique makes it far easier to submerge docks, piers, logs, sunken ships, and other "bottom" debris because the plaster will hold the debris exactly where you want it for the later pourings. You can often rest boat bottoms on this plaster or partially embed the keel of the boat in it to hold it firmly when the "water" is added.

The Shoreline

Artist's gloss medium and the resins like Envirotex have nearly opposite characteristics at the places where the "wet" material ends and the dry "shore" begins. The gloss medium is so thick that the surface of the water may actually be higher than the shore. The solution here is to brush the gloss medium along the shoreline with a paint brush, a wooden tongue depressor, or an ice-cream stick. The epoxy will pull itself up into the shoreline to produce a concave water edge. Wait until it hardens completely, then paint the shoreline with latex or Polly S paint, and, if you wish, sprinkle on some dirt, ground foam, or other texture material. If you plan to have weeds or bushes growing in the shallow water's edge, insert them into the last $\frac{1}{8}$-inch pour of epoxy or into the surface of the gloss medium before either fluid hardens.

Rapids, Waterfalls, and Other White Water

Artist's gloss medium is thick enough to be brushed over a slope as steep as about 45 degrees and to a thickness of nearly $\frac{1}{16}$ inch before it will run. You will have to experiment to determine just how much of a slope you can paint with the gloss medium, but remember that you can go back with more coats to build up the depth. In general, you will discover that if water would actually flow over the simulated rock bed of your rapid-flowing stream the gloss medium will duplicate that effect. If the slope is so steep that a waterfall would form, you will have to "build" that portion of the rapids and install it *before* pouring or brushing on the actual stream. When the gloss medium has dried completedly, brush on the faintest trace of pearl-colored fingernail polish to simulate frothing white water. Simulate the texture of the bubbling water by pocking and stirring the gloss medium just as it sets. If you want a large mass of bubbling water, such as at the foot of a waterfall, crumple up cellophane, pin it in place with straight pins (but leave the heads sticking up $\frac{1}{4}$ inch), and pour gloss medium over the cellophane. When the first layer dries, pull the pins out and add another layer of gloss medium. Finally, add touches of pearl fingernail polish.

The simplest way to create a waterfall is to use the Color-Rite kit (Fig. 7–4) made of plastic that can be cut to any length or width. For smaller waterfalls, paint three to six layers of gloss medium onto a clean plate of glass. When the gloss medium dries, scrape it from the glass with a single-edge razor blade. Cut the material into strips and brush on a thin series of white flow lines with Polly S paints. Cover the Polly S with another coat of gloss medium *after* you have glued the simulated waterfalls or rivulets into the streambed with gloss medium (Fig. 7–5). Add a few light streaks of pearl fingernail polish after the last coat of gloss medium is dry.

Fig. 7–4 The Color-Rite plastic waterfall with fluffed cotton to simulate spray at the bottom of each falls. Or use cellophane and gloss medium instead of cotton.

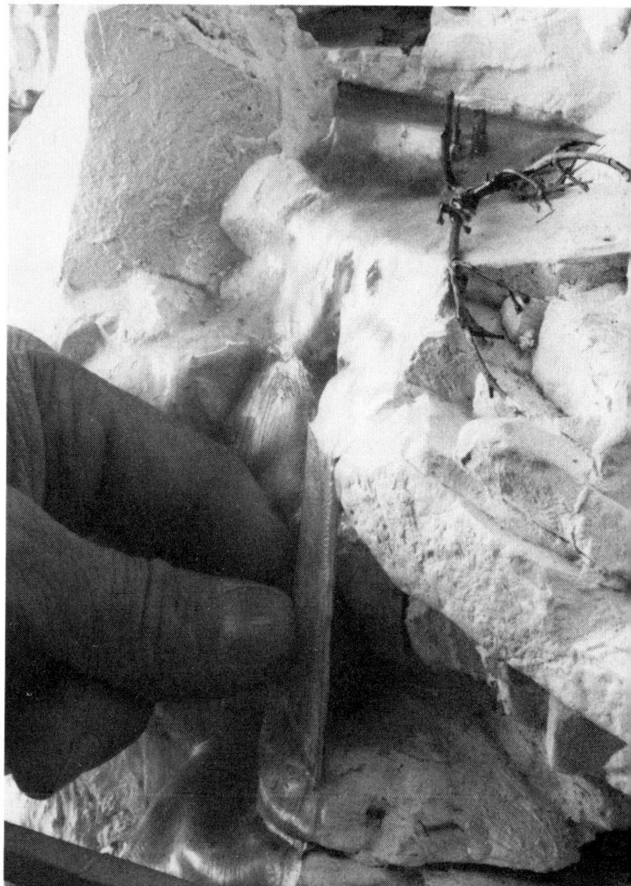

Fig. 7–5 Thick slabs of artist's gloss medium, colored with streaks of white and pearl, are glued to the sides of rocks to simulate falls.

Seascapes

The oceans, seas, and Great Lakes are some of the most difficult portions of the real world to bring down to a miniature scene with any degree of realism. One of the major problems with such large bodies of water is that the horizon is nearly impossible to duplicate because of the unlimited variety of viewing positions available to anyone admiring your model. Movie and television special-effects experts can make a credible ocean from a swimming pool-sized body of water because they control the horizon by controlling the camera angle. The modeler, however, must be prepared to slice through the "ocean" along at least one side of any scene and hope that the boat or shoreline will distract the viewer away from the missing horizon. Nevertheless, the seascape-building technique is well worth developing, since most miniature ships look more realistic resting in an ocean or harbor diorama.

You can learn from the mistakes of generations of modelers and not model any water effects that are deeper than about two inches. Real water becomes murky at that depth. The trick is to include enough dye in the lower depths of the water so that the bottom appears to be some undefinable depth below the visible depth. A depth of just one inch of simulated water is enough to convey the feeling; you can make the water deeper to avoid cutting the hull of a full-hull model ship by pouring plastic water up to the ship's waterline. In some cases, you might want to extend partially submerged ships, anchor lines, or broken piers as far as two inches below the surface. If you must have deep water, the best technique for creating it involves two materials: one to build up the depth to the *lowest* ebb point of any waves, and the second to mold and shape the waves.

To use decoupage epoxy for deep water with a cut through water at the edge of the table or diorama, you must build a temporary watertight dam to create the vertical edge for the epoxy water. Six to ten layers of plastic Baggies can be sandwiched between the baseboard for the diorama or the edge of the model railroad benchwork and a piece of perfectly flat plywood. The extra layers of Baggies should provide plenty of sealing surface to prevent the fluid epoxy from running out. Be sure to stretch the Baggies tight and flat so they won't be captured inside the resin. You can spray their surface with a light spray of silicone lubricant, which acts as a mold release. The Baggies can be pulled away from the hardened vertical edge of the resin. Mix only enough resin to form a layer between $\frac{1}{8}$ and $\frac{1}{4}$ inch thick and allow that layer to harden for 48 hours before pouring in the next $\frac{1}{8}$- to $\frac{1}{4}$-inch layer. Repeat the pours and the 48-hour setting periods between each pour, until the resin is as deep as you desire.

Boat and Ship Scenes

A diorama with a ship or boat cutting through the simulated water with a series of bow waves and a frothy wake is exciting to see in pictures, but it is seldom realistic in real life. You expect those waves to be "frozen" in a photograph, but you also expect them to be moving when you see them in three dimensions, even as a model diorama. This same logic applies to rolling breakers or waves like those in Tom Knapp's N-scale harbor scene (Fig. 7–6 and the color section). For

Fig. 7–6 The waves on Tom Knapp's N-scale model of a California beach were shaped in plaster of paris and painted blue-green and white.

maximum realism, then, limit your dioramas with ships to harbor scenes or even dry dock scenes where the lack of water action is not noticeable.

For that dramatic water-in-motion effect, you have two choices: Mold the actual waves in plaster, as Tom Knapp did, or use several layers of artist's gloss medium on top of the resin "depths" to build up the shapes you desire. The gloss medium is thick enough to form as much as $\frac{1}{4}$-inch high wave peaks while it is still wet. With four or five applications, you can create just about any bow wave or wake froth effect (Fig. 7–7). If you mold the waves in plaster, brush on three or four coats of artist's gloss medium to give a waterlike gloss and depth. The major difference between the two processes is that you can dye the lower layers of resin to create more realistic depths to the water, whereas using plaster waves demands that you color the plaster surface alone. Use the same techniques for creating rapids and other white water.

The Beach

The frothy water washed ashore by waves helps to hide the actual bottom of any beach. This means that you have the freedom either to model the beach bottom to where the ocean is an inch or so deep and pour in the Envirotex or to shape the ocean in plaster using the artist's gloss medium techniques. Simulated sand or rocks must be applied before the final coat of resin or gloss medium. Do not run sifted sand so far into the "water" that the resin can cover it, since air bubbles probably will appear. To be safe, model the shape of the beach in Hydrocal or plaster and paint it the proper color. You can also add any rocks or stones larger than about $\frac{1}{4}$ inch. Then pour in the resin until it reaches to within $\frac{1}{16}$ inch of the *depth* of the water on the shore. Now you can apply the sand using the same techniques for applying real dirt in Chapter 5. Sift the sand through a tea strainer, then through a number 100-sieve brass plumber's screen, and use only the particles that pass through the tea strainer but not through the 100 sieve. When the Bonding Agent that holds the sand dries, apply the final $\frac{1}{16}$ inch of *depth* using artist's gloss medium.

The Harbor

Harbors are usually full of activity in real life, and these actitivites can be modeled with a high degree of credibility. A viewer expects

Fig. 7–7 Dave Simpson's 12 × 12-inch diorama of a scratch-built N-scale railroad car ferry has epoxy "water" complete with bow waves and wake.

Fig. 7–8 The harbor on Willard Jones's HO-scale railroad has clear epoxy "water" with a removable freight-car-carrying barge.

some pause in any work activity, so a frozen-in-time diorama or model-railroad harbor scene will be more realistic than one where the boats or ships are *supposed* to be moving. The most important element of the harbor scene is just what you hope it will be—your ship models. When you create a diorama with the ship moving through choppy seas or kicking up a bow wave, the viewer's attention is focused more on the water than on the diorama. The harbor scene allows use of the proven theatrical techniques in Chapters 1 and 8 as well as most of the chapters that follow.

For the model railroader, the harbor can be a perfect source of freight shipments of almost any kind. The car ferry (Figs. 7–7 and 7–8), another harbor-based industry, can provide for the shipment of a half-dozen model freight cars carrying a great variety of products. Stone walls and pilings are typical "scenery" for harbors. The pilings can be simple wooden dowels with extra grain scraped into them with the blade of a razor saw. For simulated barnacles, attach some fine grind foam with artist's matte medium and color it a seaweed gray/green. Remember, too, that harbors appear on large rivers, long lakes, the Great Lakes, and in river deltas as well as oceans. A barge scene would be equally suitable in a scene that depicts New Jersey, Missouri, British Columbia, Alaska and a host of other locations.

Chapter 8

Close-Up Credibility and Superdetails

Perhaps the best definition of superdetails is the "great overlooked obvious." For example, you cannot build a realistic model of a modern interstate highway without including tar-filled cracks and paper debris along the roadside. Similarly, no forest scene is complete without fallen branches. A superdetail falls into the general category of "debris." If you train yourself to look at a real life scene or a photograph of a historical scene and pick out the debris, you will begin to develop the skill that makes any model scene into a realistic work of art. Debris usually is not considered pretty enough to be included in a model, but any model scene that lacks debris lacks the most important *living* element of any real-life scene.

Basic Clutter

The clutter that surrounds a scene *defines* the scene. You won't find many fallen tree limbs beneath trees in a park; the freshly mown grass is what defines the scene as a park. Fallen tree limbs, dead leaves, and a random array of weeds, grasses, and general ground contours define a natural setting, the *opposite* of a park scene. The wooden washtub, rough-hewn pitchfork, and rope-trussed bird define the log hut as that of a peasant in George DeWolfe's diorama (Fig. 8–2 and the color section). The piles of wheels, gears, and other mechanical clutter define Bob Brown's narrow-gauge engine house (Fig. 8–1) as a "backwoods" scene. Bob's ¼-inch-scale (On3 and On2) scenes were among the earlier dioramas to emphasize the importance of clutter as well as weathering. Clutter can also date the scene; fresh concrete suggests a new

Fig. 8–1 Bob Brown's O-scale engine house captures the look of a backwoods branch-line operation.

highway, while jagged tar strips and roughened textures suggest aged concrete. A street scene with only sidewalks has no life until parking meters, mailboxes, awnings, streetlights, lights for signs, curbs, gutters, drains, manholes, and fire hydrants are added. Re-creating any scene in miniature will force you to see clutter that you never noticed before, and adding that clutter will give the scene a true-to-life effect.

Fig. *8–2* George DeWolfe's 1/35-scale diorama depicts a peasant's hut.

Handmade Debris and Litter

In the previous chapters, warnings have been given about the unnatural appearance of dyed sawdust, real rocks, and untreated lichen. The clutter suggested in this chapter is really just another form of *texture*. Clutter, debris, and litter provide evidence of human activity. With the exceptions of parks and new highways, every other portion of the scenes we model will likely be covered with dead limbs, natural erosion, naturally broken and man-cut tree stumps, old fences and other discarded scraps of lumber, tangles of barbed wire or old cable, empty cans and barrels, and so on. The modeler is blessed with an incredible array of commercial products to make it easier to duplicate debris texture, but most debris can be made from things around the house, including the fine twig ends of hedges and weeds, nylon sewing thread, broken wooden matches, pieces of wooden toothpicks and meat skewers (to represent cans and short pieces of pipe), leftover bits of wood or plastic from any kit, crumpled bits of aluminum foil, and foil pressed over a coarse metal file (to make corrugations like those near the upper center of Figure 8–1), and bits of facial tissue folded and painted to simulate tarps or empty cloth sacks. In addition to the usual earth textures, you will want to add small piles and spills of coal, sand, and railroad track ballast. Firms like Bachmann, Campbell, Highball, John's Lab, Life-Like, and Woodland Scenics make all three of these textures in a variety of sizes and colors. You can also use real coal, sand, or ballast that has been crushed with a hammer inside a cloth bag and sifted through a 40-sieve-size tea strainer.

Off-the-Shelf Clutter and Debris

The Walthers' *HO Railroad Catalog* and JMC International's *Source Book*, Volume 4, contain hundreds of scale-size metal castings for details like electrical meters, parking meters, hand tools, buckets, cans, barrels, industrial wheels, gears, and pulleys, downspouts, pipe and pipe fittings, and just about anything else you might find in a hardware store. All of these are suitable for models between about 1/160 and 1/40 scale. There is also a wide selection of different sizes of chain, hooks, and, from Vintage Reproductions, even scale-size cable. Don't forget scale-size railroad spikes, short lengths of rail or structural angle iron and I-beams, tie plates, rail joiners, and scale nuts and bolts, all listed in the Walthers and JMC catalogs. These items are suitable for military dioramas as well as for railroad, dock, or other industrial senes. Military modelers will want to watch for the boxes of plastic parts and clutter in 1/76, 1/48, and 1/35 scales from the same firms that make tanks and other armored vehicles. Railroad modelers, especially those working in S or 0 scales, should take a good look at these military diorama details; there are some real bargains in details such as barrels, tools, wheels, tires, fences, and even scale-model people.

Chooch produces what must be the ultimate in easy-to-use debris or clutter texture—one-piece precolored and weathered epoxy moldings of entire piles of junk (Fig. 8–3). Chooch offers loads of "Scrap" and "Junk" for Athearn and Roundhouse 40- and 50-foot gondolas

Fig. 8–3 Chooch's HO-scale "Piles of Junk" (left) and loads of junk and scrap for HO-scale gondolas (right) are prepainted epoxy castings.

(Fig. 12–5, right). These can be used as is for piles of junk around any industrial scene in just about any scale. The firm also has "Assorted Junk Piles" in both HO (1/87) scale (Fig. 12–5, left) and 0 (1/48) scale. The piles of junk can be cut apart to produce six various-sized individual piles. Use a coping saw or a jeweler's saw to cut the castings. The 40- and 50-foot HO-scale gondola loads can also be cut into several shorter piles. When you install this debris in the scenery, mask it carefully until the surrounding dirt and ground foam is in place and the Bonding Agent has dried. You can sift on more loose dirt and green foam to simulate weeds and add some foxtail or cattail "weeds" (see Figs. 5–8 and 5–10) to add incredible realism to the Chooch castings.

Buildings as Scenery

Before you create your own scene, take the time to study similar real world scenes so that you can identify what elements of the scene, such as building height or texture or a balance between tall and short and old and new, make real-world scenes exciting.

Nearly every real world structure offers some outside evidence of its function. These finer details were once reserved for contest models, but today many of them are included even in inexpensive plastic kits. Some of the most important details are the evidence of that structure's links with the rest of the world. Be sure to include at least one source of electrical power in the form of a nearby pole, if not the actual wires leading to the insulator on the structure itself. Be sure also that some type of path or road leads to every door.

Selective Compression

No model railroader is foolish enough to attempt to re-create any more than a tiny fraction of a real mountain in miniature. Even if reduced to N ($\frac{1}{160}$) scale, a relatively low 500-foot hill would soar nearly 3 feet above the table. Wise modelers duplicate the proper angle of the slopes and the correct-scale textures and reproduce nearly full-size trees in the foreground. The trees near the top of the mountains and near the background are reduced in size, getting ever smaller as they get closer to the crest of the hill or the backdrop in a "forced perspective." This same principle can be applied when reducing any real-world structure to a suitable size for a model railroad. With the exception of relatively small one- or two-story buildings, *any* large building can be reduced to help conserve space without noticeably affecting its proportions. Figure 8–4 shows how the Holly Sugar Plant in Santa Ana, California, can be reduced by half for a full-scale model. Selective compression does *not* reduce the size of doors or windows; it merely reduces the building's overall *proportions*. The building retains its character even in reduced scale. The technique can be used for bridges as well.

An actual factory

A. Four stories high.
B. Five bays wide.
C. Twelve bays wide.
D. Four bays wide.
E. Three stories high.

A model factory
reduced to scale by
selective compression

A. Three stories high.
B. Four bays wide.
C. Eight bays wide.
D. Two bays wide.
E. Two stories high.

Fig. 8–4 The technique of selective compression reduces the size of a real structure while retaining its proportions and scale-size windows and doors.

A Firm Foundation

The most glaring flaw in most model buildings is the dark, shadowed gap between the foundation and the earth or pavement that surrounds it. The model looks as though it had been dropped in place by some giant (which of course it was). The gap around the base of any building must be hidden, and the building must rest in the scene with all four walls perfectly horizontal. Many otherwise realistic scenes are spoiled by buildings that tilt and lean at right angles to the ground rather than at right angles to the *horizon*.

Buildings must be planned *before* the scenery is in place. Use blocks of wood or scraps of cardboard to mount the building supports so that they are secure and perfectly level. Use a carpenter's bubble-type level *every* time to be sure. You can then drape plaster of Hydrocal scenery everywhere but directly on the building site. Avoid any chance of getting the hills too close by tracing a bright red outline of the building with a grease pencil. Stop the plaster application when you're within $\frac{1}{8}$ inch or so of the building outline. The building can be "buried" with an additional application of plaster or by installing the building before you install the ground-cover textures; these textures will fill in any gaps around the base. If you want to avoid trapping the structure in plaster and Bonding Agent, coat the base of the building with Krasel's "Micro Mask," a liquid mask that can be peeled off when dry, and apply a touch of Vaseline over it. When the texturing is completely dry, remove the building, peel off the mask, and replace the building. The techniques for "planting" the abutments and lowest beams of bridges in Chapter 3 will work just as well with mines and other structures on pilings.

The City as Scenery

Too few modelers consider urban scenes worth re-creating. The city, however, provides one of the most practical means of camouflaging the necessary disappearance of the tracks on most model railroads. Trains can simply disappear behind buildings without the need to make excuses for too many tunnels. Hills and mountains consume a considerable amount of scarce table space because of their slopes; it takes at least a foot of table space for every foot of elevation on a realistic moutain slope. The result of this hillside problem is that modelers use too many rock cliffs on their railroads. City buildings rise vertically, with the only necessary ground space being the streets, curbs, and loading docks. The most effective use of the city as scenery is on the HO-scale model railroad of the Sverna Park Model Railroad Club near Baltimore, Maryland. Dr. Logan Holtgrewe and the other club members have created a city scene that uses every trick, from selective compression to "flats" to cutout portions of calendar photos as flats. The entire city occupies only about 4 × 12 feet. About 4 × 6 feet of it is visible in Figures 8–5 and 8–6, about the same as most average-size model railroads. Dr. Holtgrewe built most of the buildings from scratch, but there are nearly a hundred HO-scale structure kits that could be used to duplicate the effect.

Fig. 8–5 Dr. Logan Holtgrewe scratch-built the foreround buildings and used cutout color photographs of real structures as flats on this Sverna Park Model Railroad Club layout.

Buildings as Flats

The relatively high level of the track (about 48 inches from the floor) allows the structures in the Sverna Park city scene to reach *above* the eye level of even the tallest spectator. This means that there is no need to consider a horizon (see Chapter 9) and, more important, that only the fronts of the buildings are visible. Because the structures are placed

Fig. 8–6 A bird's-eye view of the Sverna Park city scene reveals that nearly all the buildings are flats. A few water tanks and chimneys suggest roofs.

close together, as in any real city, the view of the sides is blocked by adjacent buildings. The roofs are not visible because they stretch above eye level. The net result is that most of the structures need to be modeled only as fronts, or "flats" (Fig. 8–5 and 8–6). If you use kits for the structures, only one wall has to be supported; the ends and back wall can be located elsewhere or joined to the front wall to increase the length or height of the structure. The bird's-eye view of the Sverna Park scene in Figure 8–6 reveals that little layout space is occupied by the buildings; most of the benchwork is covered with tracks hidden by the flats but accessible by reaching over the tops of the flats. The technique allows you to fill a large area with structures with no more effort or time than filling the same area with hills or mountains. More views of the Sverna Park scenery appear in the color section and in Volume 3 of *The Model Railroading Handbook*.

People and Animals

Diorama builders usually prefer to have people in active poses, whereas model railroaders can create more realistic scenes with people in static or resting poses, sitting, leaning, or just standing. There are two obvious differences in these approaches. The proponents of

Fig. 8–7 Most of the figures in this city scene, created by Magnuson Models to display its structures, are in static poses.

"active" poses feel they are creating a frozen moment in history. The true essence of most military modelers' dioramas is this stop-action effect, but the effect does not work as well in three dimensions as it does in two. A scene where you cannot tell whether the figures are "frozen in action" or simply resting is the most enjoyable to view. In any case, the "resting" poses are far easier to make realistic. Action

Fig. 8–8 The bases of the figures in Magnuson's city scene have been removed and pins stuck into the legs and platform to support them.

poses usually work for museum modelers, but most of us amateurs lack the skills and experience of the pros.

Modifying Ready-Made People

Most HO (1/87) and O (1/48) scale cast-metal and molded plastic people and animals have a built-in or glued-on base to keep them upright. The first step in making them realistic is to saw a molded-on base away with a razor saw. If the base is glued on, you can probably dissolve the glue joint with a half-dozen applications of liquid cement for plastics. When the base is free, allow the cement to dry for about a week because it may have softened the plastic. To support the figures, insert a straight pin through the bottom of the foot (or hoof or paw). Use a number 70-size drill bit in a pin vise and drill a hole. When the

Fig. 8–9 These Preiser HO-scale figures have been repainted to make them the focal point of a foreground scene in Magnuson's diorama.

pin is in place, cut off the head with a pair of diagonal cutters so that about $\frac{1}{8}$ to $\frac{1}{4}$ inch protrudes from the figure. This length can usually be pushed directly into wooden platforms and plaster scenery, but you may also have to drill the pin hole in Hydrocal, plastic, or metal surfaces. The pin will hold the figure upright, but it is flexible enough to bend it slightly. In most scenes, the figures can be removed from their pinholes, which are not noticeable enough to detract from the scene. All of the model figures, from N-scale workmen to the 1/35-scale plastic infantrymen, have truly incredible details and relief, from the faces to the clothing with its tucks and folds. When these figures are painted, though, they somehow lose much of their three-dimensional effect. The solution is simple. Add extra shadow detail to the recesses and touch a bit of lighter color to the high spots to give them highlights. When you mix the paints for the face, for example, drop some of the paint onto a piece of glass with an eye dropper. Add a small puddle of a darker matching color and a small puddle of off-white (Fig. 8–10). Paint the face with skin color (Reference Card 22).

Fig. 8–10 Mix lighter and darker shades on a glass palette (left) and blend shadow and highlights directly on the figure with a number 00 paint brush.

Three-Step Skin-Tone Painting

Step 1:
Paint all flesh areas with basic skin tone

Polly S Paint
1 part Flesh PF23
1 part Reefer White PR11

Step 2:
Brush on overall wash of shadow color to fill in hollows and creases in skin areas

1 part Harvest Gold PF42
19 parts water
4 drops dishwashing detergent per pint

Step 3:
Dry-brush highlights such as cheeks, forehead, chin, backs of fingers, and wrists

1 part Earth Yellow PF41
or 1 part Flesh PF23
or 1 part Mud PR83
9 parts water
4 drops dishwashing detergent per pint

While the paint is still wet, use a number 0000 brush or a brush with just two or three bristles to add darker tones to the recessed areas around the eyes and neck and lighter tones to raised areas like cheekbones. For 1/48-scale or larger figures, paint the eyes first; for smaller-scale figures, paint the eyes after the flesh tones dry. Use a wash of brown to highlight the mouth. When painting a dozen or more figures, use the three-step technique on Reference Card 22 to speed up the process. The key to this technique is to highlight the shading and molded-in details on the figure when a wash of a darker tone is applied. The wash will blend nicely into the recesses while running clear of any raised areas. A nearly dry brush-tip touch of a lighter color will provide a similarly quick highlight for cheeks and other raised areas. For well-worn clothing on military figures or construction crews, add Steps 4 and 5 of the weathering technique in Chapter 10 (Reference Card 24).

Most domestic and farm animals are available prepainted in N, HO, and O scales from AHM, Bachmann, Dyna-Models, LaBelle, Campbell/Weston, Kibri, Merten, and Preiser. Durango Press, Lytler & Lytler, Atlas, Grandt, Magnuson, LaBelle, MDK, and Preiser offer unpainted figures. The Walthers and JMC International catalogs illustrate most of figures available in the smaller scales. In many military vehicle sets, 1/48 and 1/35 scale figures are included or sold as "accessory" packs. Few of the painted figures are done with enough neatness to be realistic. The Campbell/Weston figures are fine out of the box, and the Merten and Preiser figures are passable; other painted figures should be touched up with washes to accent their colors and a coat of Testors "Dullcote" applied to kill the glossy paint. The prepainted animals are more acceptable than most prepainted human figures. However, nearly all of the animals can benefit from a "dry-brushing" coat of a slightly darker shade to emphasize the textures of hair. The dry-brushing technique requires that you barely touch the extreme ends of the brush bristles to the paint. The paint is then dabbed onto the model with very light strokes to produce hairlike streaks of colors. For highlighting humans and clothing, the dry-brush technique is altered to produce a dabbing on-off stroke with the tip of the brush. A final wash of 19 parts water to 1 part Polly S Roof Brown (with 4 drops of dishwashing detergent added per pint of fluid) will help to accent the molded-in detail on any animal figure.

Chapter 9

Backdrops, Perspective, and Lighting

The primary purpose of a backdrop behind a model railroad or diorama is to convey the feeling that the scene extends to the horizon and beyond. The single most important element is the horizon because that is where our eye tells us the scene ends. No large diorama and no model railroad scene will be credible without a horizon positioned at or above the eye level of the average viewer. This means that the benchwork supporting the model railroad or the shelf supporting the diorama must be high enough so that the hills or structures along the rear of the scene are within six inches or so of the height of the viewer's eyes.

The Horizon

Chunk Spinks's HO-scale modular layout is built in an "inside corner," a portion of a model railroad that fits snugly inside the corner of a room (Figs. 9–1 and 9–2). Nearly every item in his module, from the Woodland Scenics ground-foam grass to the buildings to the HO West! backdrop is a commercial product. Chuck blended these elements together to create some very credible close-up details, like the cracked concrete street and the dirt alley to the right of the scene. He also did some careful color matching. The brickwork on the plastic kit structures was painted in about the same shades of red as the two-dimensional buildings that Tom Daniels painted on the master scene for the HO West! printing process. Chuck was also wise enough to know that the backdrop should be curved around the corner to camouflage the actual joint between the two corner walls. The walls still have that joint, of course, but the HO West! backdrop, mounted on a curved piece of Masonite, hides the actual corner. He also aligned the backdrop so that it would appear to be a continuation of the modeled street when viewed from about 9 inches above the table (Fig. 9–2). When viewed from about 2 feet above the table, which places the layout at about a conventional table height of 30 inches, the scene is far more toylike. The lesson here is that the layout itself should be

Fig. 9–1 Chuck Spinks's HO-scale modular model railroad is a 4 × 4-foot inner corner with a curved HO West! backdrop.

Fig. 9–2 The city in Chuck Spinks's module is more realistic when viewed from near the track level rather than from overhead.

placed near eye level for maximum realism. One of the advantages of a model railroad, particularly one built on a shelf for an around-the-wall layout, is that it fills the viewer's peripheral vision on both sides. The effect is the same as a wide-angle movie screen to a viewer seated in the front of the theater. You are drawn directly into the scene, so you automatically feel that you are part of that imaginary world. Figure 9–3 portrays the ideal method of building and lighting a model railroad. First, the layout is placed high enough so that the mountains extend almost to eye level. Remember, the real horizon is at eye level.

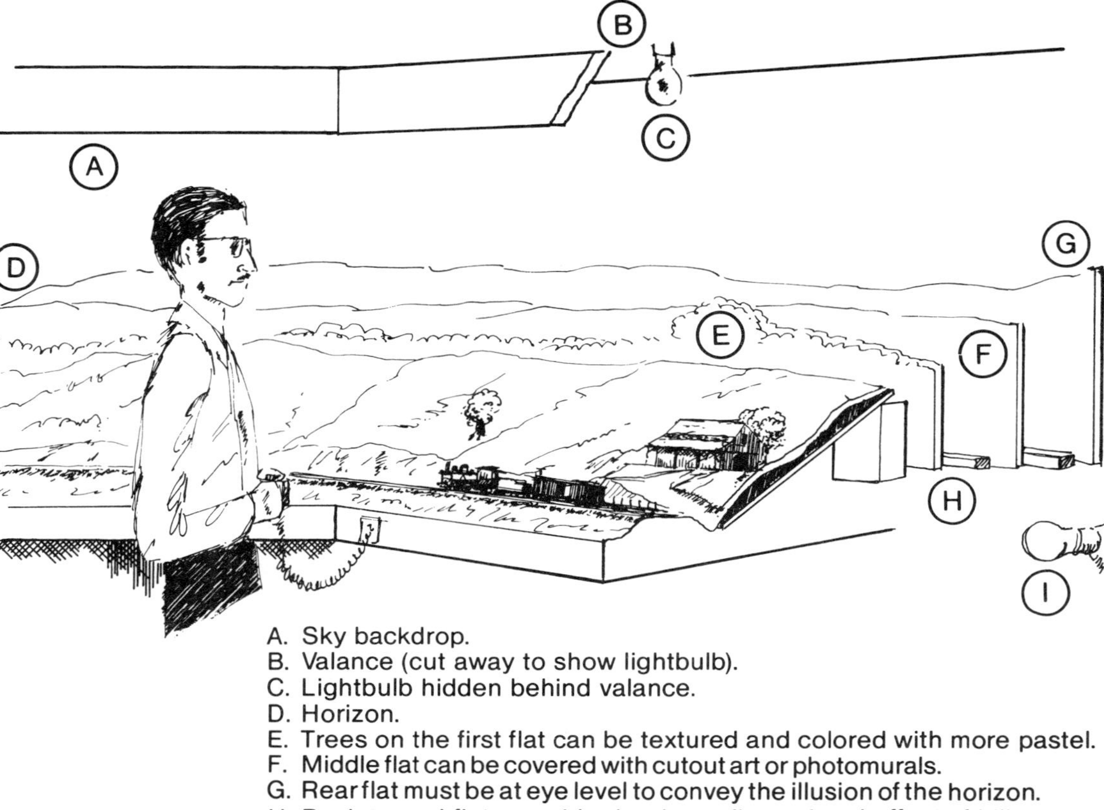

A. Sky backdrop.
B. Valance (cut away to show lightbulb).
C. Lightbulb hidden behind valance.
D. Horizon.
E. Trees on the first flat can be textured and colored with more pastel.
F. Middle flat can be covered with cutout art or photomurals.
G. Rear flat must be at eye level to convey the illusion of the horizon.
H. Background flats provide the three-dimensional effect of hills.
I. Lighting for the horizon is placed below the scenery and flats.

Fig. 9–3 A cutaway view of the optimum arrangement for a shelf-style model railroad. The three background flats are spaced only an inch or two apart. They are staggered here to show their shapes and the 1×1 supporting blocks.

Backdrop Colors

	Polly S Color	Glidden Interior Latex Paint
Sky Blue		
Overhead at 10,000 feet	1 part Blue PR58 1 part Sea Blue PF31	Blue Indigo
Horizon near sea level	Sea Blue PF31	Bobby
Clouds		
White (tops)	Reefer White PR11	White
Blue/gray (shadows)	Federal Blue PF26	Hudson Bay

Note: To simulate overcast skies or hazy seacoasts, blend backdrop with an overhead color near Sea Blue or Bobby, blending to a mixture of blue-gray and white at eye level, the actual horizon of your scene.

When you are relatively close to any mountains or hills, they mask the true horizion. The model scene must reproduce this effect by having the mountain peaks extend as high as you would *expect* them to.

The scene in Figure 9–3 is one of rolling foothills; the distant hills extend only to eye level to *imply* that you could see the valley *beyond*. If the scene depicted true mountains, the background flats or hills would have to be positioned at least a foot higher. In fact, if the tabletop or track level is at about chest level, the mountains would extend far enough above the horizon so that "flats" or painted mountains would be unnecessary; only a distant blue-sky backdrop need be installed. This is one reason why mountain scenes are so popular with modelers. With some thoughtful planning and construction, you can incorporate the lessons of Figure 9–3 and make rolling hills or farmland as realistic as mountains. The background flats would have to be placed only an inch or two apart to give a three-dimensional effect.

Blue-Sky Backdrops

Every model railroad should be constructed so that the walls of the room or any visible areas behind the layout are completely hidden with a sky backdrop that extends from the tabletop all the way to the ceiling. Some museum dioramas even curve the vertical blue-sky backdrop over to the roof of the room, but that's not worth the trouble on a model railroad; the viewer's eye should be directed at the scene, not at the ceiling. If your model railroad has a rear edge of 8 feet or less, consider using a single piece of $\frac{1}{8}$-inch hardboard like Masonite. This material can be curved for inside corners (Fig. 9–1) if it is supported every 6 inches or so with wooden blocks along the backs of the horizontal edges. For most model railroads, however, the backdrop must be much longer; even a 4 × 8-foot layout will usually have a backdrop with one curved corner connecting one 4-foot and one 8-foot edge to require at least an 11-foot-long backdrop. The best material for such backdrops is the least expensive grade of linoleum or vinyl floor covering. If you can find 36-inch-wide hall runners, use them; if not, buy the 6-foot-wide material and split it into two 3-foot pieces. The only limit on the length of this linoleum is the amount of weight you can lift—a 25-foot roll is about maximum. The most likely sources for 36-inch linoleum are stores like Sears, Penneys, or Montgomery Ward.

Since the linoleum can be ordered in almost any length, you won't have to camouflage the seams with patches that will eventually crack; you would, however, have to patch the Masonite. Avoid flowery patterns of linoleum because the pattern may show through as shadows. The colors on Reference Card 23 allow you to blend true sky blue at the top of the backdrop with a lighter blue at the horizion by mixing in more white as you paint the backdrop from top to bottom. Apply the paint with a 4-inch-wide roller and paint the entire length with each color mix, blending the ever-lighter shades of blue down to the horizon (Fig. 9–4).

Photomurals and Painted Backdrops

There is some disagreement, even among museum diorama builders, as to whether a photomural or a painted backdrop is more realistic. The problem with the photomural is that it is more realistic than the foreground. This can be overcome if you have the nerve to spray a light wash of gray-white over the expensive photomural with an air-brush. The wash lends the misty look of faraway scenes and softens the harsh colors in the mural. If you wish to make photomurals from your own color negatives, ask your local camera shops for prices. Expect to pay several hundred dollars for even a 4-foot photo in four colors. The best alternatives are the printed photomurals for model railroads from Vollmer (a city scene) and Faller (superb mountains, foothills, and farmland). Some wallpaper shops also carry photomurals for interior decorating. Some of these murals may have scenes that are the proper size and style for model railroad, but they are also in the hundred-dollar-and-up price range.

The most effective painted backdrops are those sold under the HO West! and Detail Associates labels by most model railroad shops, as well as by Walthers and JMC International. The Detail Associates backdrops are designed to be used as profile cutouts; you cut out the outlines of the tops of the hills, mountains, or structures with scissors and glue them to the backdrop with rubber cement. It's more realistic if you actually use these profiles as flats by gluing them to stiff plastic "For Sale" signs or pieces of Masonite hardboard. The plastic or Masonite should first be cut to match the upper outline of the hill, mountain, or structure profile (see Figures 8–5 and 8–6). Cut them about $\frac{1}{8}$ inch smaller so that the paper cutout protrudes that much above the plastic or Masonite. This hides the thickness of the plastic or Masonite. (Do not use cardboard; it will warp from changes in humidity.) Color

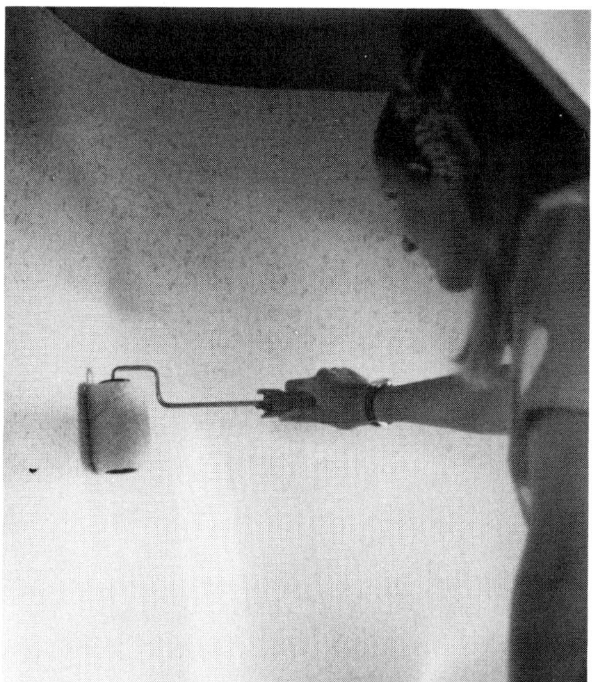

Fig. 9–4 With a narrow roller, paint the deep blue of the upper sky to blend gradually into a white-blue near the horizon. Twist the roller for puffy clouds, and use just a trace of paint for horizontal wisps.

the white edges of the cutouts with felt-tipped pens to match the scenes.

The flats can be positioned just an inch or two in front of the sky-blue linoleum backdrop to provide a three-dimensional effect to the horizon (see Fig. 9–3). This technique can be used effectively by cutting out individual hills and mountains from the Faller photomural backdrops. The "profile" or "flats" technique allows you to use just a single scene several times by purchasing duplicates of the scene and overlapping the hills, mountains, or structures to vary the appearance, but not the colors. If you are cramped for space, glue the cutout profiles directly to the sky backdrop. It is also possible to combine photomurals and HO West! and Detail Associates backdrops, or even to cut out calendar photos to create a single scene (see Fig. 9–6).

Forced Perspective

The basic artistic rule of perspective is that the sizes of objects appear to diminish in direct proportion to their distance from the

Fig. 9–5 Bill Peters used textured flats for the weed-covered hills and cutout color photographs and calendar art for the backdrop of this O-scale scene.

viewer. Hence, objects nearer the horizon appear to be much smaller than when viewed close up. A perfectly straight road appears to form a point as it reaches toward the horizon. You can bend this rule to make your scenes seem to be much larger by using smaller scale objects near the back of the scene. For example, if you are modeling a small town that is built on rolling hills, use HO (1/87) scale houses for the foreground with N (1/160) scale houses midway between the foreground and the sky backdrop and Z (1/220) scale houses nearest the backdrop. The sizes of the trees on Hal Riegger's N-scale layout (Fig. 9–7) seem to be the same size all the way up the mountain; in fact, the trees near the crest are only about $\frac{1}{2}$ inch high. Be sure to provide a hilltop to break any perspective that continues onto a painted

Fig. 9–6 Jack Rice's backdrop scene is a collage of Detail Associates and several HO West! backdrop scenes cut from the backdrop and cemented to a painted sky.

or photomural backdrop (Fig. 9–8). If the road is allowed to run over the crest of even a gentle hill, it can be repeated on the backdrop, but with the bottom of the road just a bit narrower to suggest that the road is further away. This technique will also be effective where rivers or streams must appear on both the backdrop and on the diorama or model railroad.

Lighting the Scene

The correct way to display an oil painting is to illuminate it with a clamp-on light above it or with a ceiling-mounted spotlight. Either spotlighting method can be used to illuminate a small diorama that

Fig. 9–7 The spirea-weed trees on Hal Riegger's N-scale layout were deliberately made smaller as they reached the top of the mountain to create a forced perspective. The mountain itself was made from broken chunks of insulating foam from a wrecked refrigerator car.

rests on a bookshelf. Lighting for a large model railroad, however, is a more complex task.

Sunlight or Bright Shade?

You have two choices of illumination for any model scene; fluorescent lighting, which produces an effect much like bright shade in the outdoors, or incandescent lighting, which produces sharp shadows similar to sunlight. Fluorescent lighting is more cost-efficient, but it can produce a negative psychological effect on the viewer. Just as

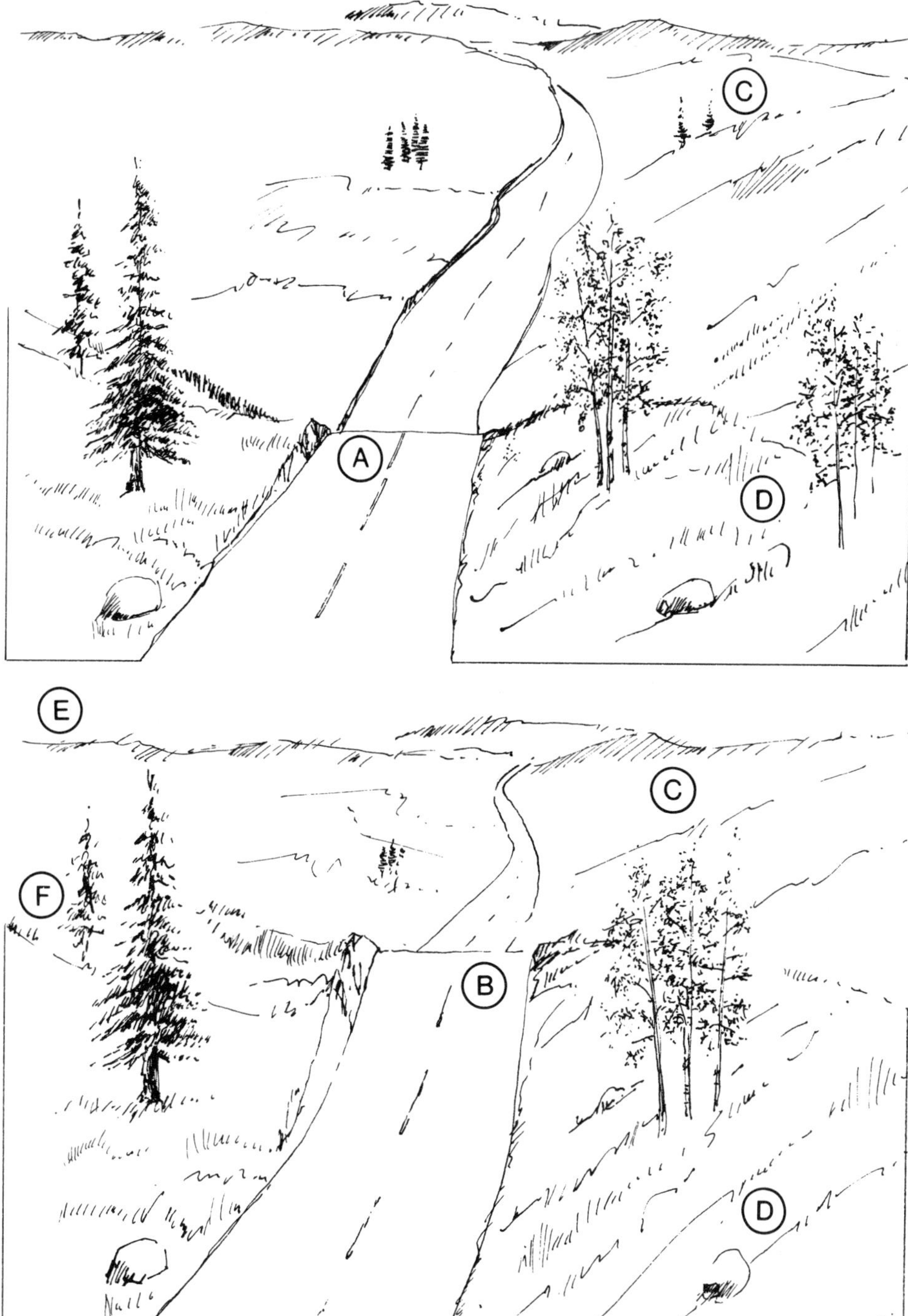

A. End of modeled road should not abut painted or photographed road; impossible to disguise joint.
B. Modeled road disappears over crest of hill, then reappears in reduced width to suggest perspective.
C. Painted or photo backdrop.
D. Modeled scenery.
E. Painted horizon near eye level.
F. Top of scenery may be below eye level.

Fig. 9–8 The "incorrect" (top) and "correct" (bottom) methods of leading a three-dimensional road (or river) onto the painted image of the backdrop road.

Fig. 9–9 Ceiling-mounted spotlights and backdrop lights behind the valance illuminate this shelf-style model railroad built to exhibit Chama Timber Company's readymade trees.

cloudy days can be depressing, so can fluorescent lighting. If your model depicts an abandoned mine or a battle scene, fluorescent lighting may produce the precise effect you are searching for. Winter or late fall scenes (see Chapter 11) can also be more effective when viewed under fluorescent lighting.

The colors and shadows of a model scene illuminated by incandescent lighting have an added warmth that makes its slightly higher cost worth the trouble. Small 50-watt miniature floodlight bulbs are relatively inexpensive to burn compared to fluorescent lighting of equal intensity, and they produce an excellent shadow effect. Remember, shadows help to define river details, the grain in scale wood, and the textures of rocks, dirt, grass, weeds, and clutter. Textures are considerably more defined by the shadows of incandescent lighting. Thus, they appear more realistic to most viewers. Lighting shops sell a va-

Fig. 9–10 The curve in the corner of this linoleum background is just visible, as are the 1 × 3 supports for the linoleum and the valance to the ceiling that hides the lights from the viewer.

riety of inexpensive fixtures that can be hidden behind valances for mounting 50-watt floodlights. Some decorative swivel lamps and reflectors also will accept these bulbs. The lighting fixtures can then be matched to the decor of a formal den or study.

Backlighting the Horizon

The most important position for any lighting system for illuminating models is one where the light is directed from either over or from behind the viewer's head. This direct lighting is necessary to highlight the details on the models. What many model railroaders forget, how-

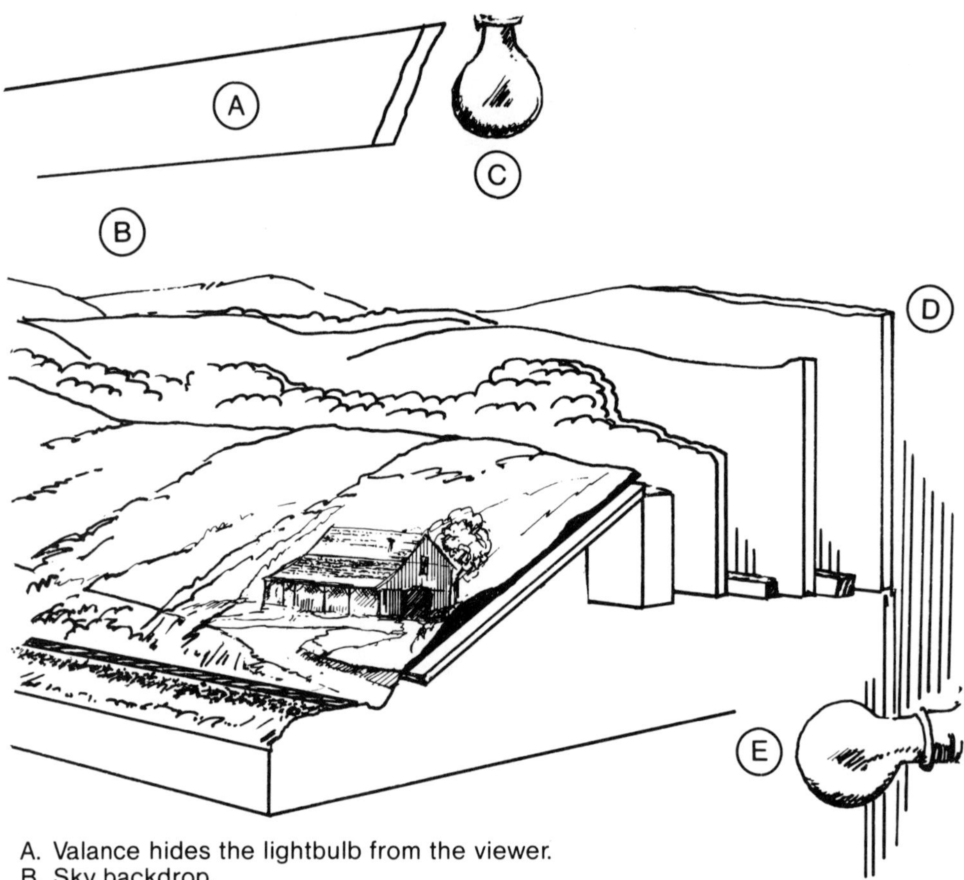

A. Valance hides the lightbulb from the viewer.
B. Sky backdrop.
C. For the effect of sunlight, the upper lights should be placed
   as close to the front of the benchwork as possible.
D. The horizon, new eye level.
E. To duplicate the brighter lighting effect of the sky and horizon,
   place the lightbulb below the layout.

Fig. 9–11 A close-up view of Figure 9–3. The foreground (upper) lighting and the
horizon lighting (lower right) exemplifies maximum "outdoor" lighting realism.

ever, is that the horizion usually appears to be brighter than the foreground. The rear edges and the backdrops of most model railroads
are almost always darker than the foreground. Much of the realism
of any scene is lost with this type of lighting. The ideal lighting positions for a model railroad are shown in Figure 9–11.

Few modelers have the foresight to leave just an inch or two open between the back of the scenery and the surface of the backdrop. The gap can be filled with one or two rows of flats (see Chapter 9) and still leave plenty of space for the passage of light from below the table. If you lack even those couple of inches, the best place for the "horizon" lighting is in the corner, where the wall and the backdrop meet the ceiling. Shield the bulbs in this area with a short valance that allows the lights to shine on the layout alone. Some modelers use this type of lighting with several ceiling-mounted spotlights shining from the access aisles above the operator's and spectators' heads (Fig. 9–12). A track-lighting system sold by lighting fixture stores would be ideal for this type of horizon lighting/aisle lighting combination. The track lighting system would allow you to move the lights for the foreground to minimize overlapping shadows or dark areas and to add or subtract lights as needed to achieve the proper effect.

Preventing or Creating Shadows

One of the major problems that a modeler faces with lighting that simulates direct sunlight is the presence of overlapping shadows from two different lights. Even the shadow from a single light is not crisp enough to match the effect of the sun. The simplest solution to the problem is to be certain that no buildings, people, telephone poles, or other vertical objects cast their shadow on a light-colored surface. You may have to repaint some light-colored concrete streets to simulate darker blacktop because the blacktop won't allow the shadows to show. Some extra dark brown weathering can be applied to any buildings or ground that are too light (see Chapter 10). A small metal valance can be cut from an aluminum pie pan and attached to the ceiling to shield just that portion of the light pattern that produces the double shadow in places where the shadow's cast is darker than the scene. One of the incidental effects of the weathering technique in Chapter 10 for buildings and figures is that the recesses of the model's texture are darkened and the faces are highlighted. These effects are precisely those produced by sunlight. These shadow and highlight effects can be carried even further on models that cannot possibly be displayed in the proper light. Use an airbrush and a wash of 19 parts Polly S dark brown or dark gray paint to 19 parts water. The shadow wash *must* be applied before the model is placed in the scene. Spray the wash from *below* the model's shape to produce a shadow effect on, for example, the bottom edges of windowsills and

Fig. 9–12 Albert Hetzel's O-scale shelf-style layout has a curved backdrop in this corner, with horizon lights hidden behind a valance and foreground lights overhead.

under the eaves of roofs, anywhere a dark shadow would appear in real life. You can carry this effect a step further and actually *paint* the darker shadow on the ground of the scene with the same wash. The technique can be especially useful when the diorama or model railroad must be illuminated with fluorescent lights.

Lighting in Miniature

Model railroad shops stock a variety of scale-model streetlights and assorted light bulbs that range in size from a flashlight bulb to the tiny bulb that's often called a "grain of rice." Most of these bulbs are about 18 volts. If you supply them with just 3 to 9 volts, you'll obtain a "scale" amount of glow and increase the life of the bulb nearly tenfold. Most model railroaders use this lighting for night scenes, but the glow from even 3 volts is still visible under most indoor lighting conditions. Jock Oliphant's mine diorama used lighting as one of many superdetails that helped earn the scene the best-display award at an annual NMRA model-building contest (Fig. 9–13). The illumination on the inside of the buildings calls attention to the interior details by making those details visible even under simulated daylight conditions.

Lighting in miniature is one of those details that must be planned when the model is being constructed so that the wires can be hidden

Fig. 9–13 The camera captures the glow of indoor and outdoor scale-size lighting as white stars on Jock Oliphant's award-winning mine diorama.

inside walls or hollow poles made from brass or aluminum tubing. The wires lead beneath the scenery to either a small transformer or a battery holder with some nicad batteries. Electronics hobby stores, such as Radio Shack or Allied Radio, can provide the proper transformer and battery holders if you show them the types of bulbs you will be using. Be sure to protect the bulbs from surrounding wood, plastic, or other flammable materials with small heat shields made from two layers of aluminum foil. The foil can also serve as a reflector for the light.

Chapter 10

The Art of Weathering

A typical example of a weather-beaten structure is an old barn, its paint so faded that the only visible color is the silvery gray of old wood. Weathering is a term coined by modelers to describe the techniques used to capture the appearance of that barn in miniature. Any man-made object that sits outdoors shows the effects of weather, so any truly realistic diorama or model railroad scene should also display some degree of weathering. Natural weathering is essentially a three-part process. Wind blows dirt onto the building, rain and dew hold that dirt in place or streak it, and the sun fades the surface. The effects of industry, like smoke stains on a chimney top or powdered concrete stains on a covered hopper car, also fall into the weathering category. The deliberate destruction from simulated bombings for military dioramas can be achieved with the same modeling techniques.

Basic Weather-Beating in Miniature

If you truly want to improve the realism of your miniatures, invest about $150 in a single-action, internal-mix airbrush, an air-pressure regulator, and an air compressor. The Walthers and JMC catalogs provide several choices, or you can find the equipment at your hobby shop or artists supply shop. The airbrush is just a miniature version of the spray guns used to paint automobiles. It produces a spray pattern that can be adjusted from something as tiny as the periods on this page to a circle about 2 inches in diameter. The advantage of the airbrush is that it gives you *complete* control over where you apply the paint, plus the ability to mix colors and washes that are not possible with aerosol cans of paint. For large painted areas, the airbrush allows you to use relatively odor-free paints like Polly S. For scenery modeling, it has the particular advantage of producing automatically the gentle shaded edges of color changes that occur so often in the real world. The gentle blend of black paint, to imitate soot stains on the chimney in Figure 10-1, could have been achieved only with an air brush. Most weathering effects in the real world are the result of wind-borne soot or dirt, and the airbrush provides a perfect method of actually duplicating *wind* as well as the color of the dirt and soot. The airbrush is not the only method of achieving weathering effects; the dark vertical stains on the power house in Figure 10–1 were done by streaking the still-fresh "weathering" colors with a number 00 paint brush and water before they could dry completely.

The Five-Step Weathering Technique

The formulas on Reference Card 24 provide short cuts for achieving the appearance of natural weather effects on virtually any model. They are applied with a brush, so if you are using an airbrush, add more water or alcohol as suggested on Reference Card 8 in Chapter 4. For that final "dusty" effect (Step 4), use artist's pastel *chalks;* the oil-base pastel sticks will not powder effectively. The chalks can be reduced to powder by rubbing them on a piece of sandpaper and catching the dust in a small jar. The pastel chalk powder can then be brushed on wherever you would normally find weathering. Never rub the chalks directly onto the model; use them only as powders. To simulate particularly dirty surfaces, such as rain-washed concrete on a covered hopper car, wet the brush before you streak on the powdered pastel chalks. The chalks produce roughly four times the color intensity when applied to a wet surface or with a wet brush. For medium effects, apply a light overspray of Testors "Dullcote" (Step 5) to seal the first pastel chalk application, then do a second application of chalk. The "Dullcote" will fade the pastel colors and soften their effect, so you may have to repeat Steps 4 and 5 two or three times to retain the effect you want and still have the protection of the final clear coat of "Dullcote."

Weathering Brick and Stone Walls

The weathering technique on Reference Card 24 makes it easy to simulate the appearance of older brick or stone walls. Many stone, brick, and wooden walls and fences in the real world have painted-on signs. The signs can be applied with dry transfers, such as Vintage

Fig. 10–1 Dr. Logan Holtgrewe's HO-scale power plant has been weathered with a subtle black shadow applied with an airbrush.

Five-Step Weathering Technique

Step 1:
For sun-faded color, mix: 3 parts Polly S color, 1 part Polly S Antique

Step 2:
To highlight shadows and seams of clothing or tents, apply wash: 1 part Polly S color, 9 parts water, 4 drops detergent per pint

Step 3:
To highlight sun- and wind-bleaching effects, use the dry-brush technique and apply: 9 parts Polly S Antique, 1 part Polly S color

Step 4:
Brush on powdered water-base artist's chalks or pastels in color closest to original shade

Step 5:
Spray entire model with a light coat of Testors "Dullcote"
Note: "Dullcote" will fade pastel chalk by several tones, so test it on a scrap first

Rocks, Weathered Wood and Brick and Stone Walls:
This technique makes it easy to superdetail rocks and cliffs, to simulate old barn wood and similar textured woods and to paint and highlight textured brick and stone walls. Use the dry-brush technique to highlight individual bricks and stones for a variegated effect.

Reproductions' "Ice" in Figures 10–3, 10–4, and 10–5. Micro Scale makes sign decals that can be used directly on the brick, stone, or wood-textured walls or fences. The decals, however, must be covered with at least six applications of decal-softening fluid like Micro Scale's "Micro Sol" so that the decal will snuggle in against the textured surface. With care, these techniques will work on paper or cardboard with printed-on brick, stone, or wood colors, but the techniques are far more effective when the texture is three-dimensional, as it is on molded-plastic or cast epoxy brick, stone, or wood walls.

Weathering Wood

Weathered wood can be made in miniature from bass or balsa wood or by scraping simulated wood grain into strips of plastic with a razor saw blade. To simulate the silver-gray color of barnwood and older wooden trestles, use the Five-Step Weathering Technique. Match the color of the real wood or a photograph of the wood to one of the colors on Reference Card 7 in Chapter 4 and proceed with the weathering technique. You may want to add an additional color for older woods. The effect of moss on the north side of the wood can be simulated by spraying on a wash of the Sage Green weed and foliage color from Reference Card 16 in Chapter 5, mixing in a total of 19 parts water to 1 part Polly S Avocado and applying the wash with an airbrush. On older weathered buildings, some of the planks will probably have broken under the weight of winter snows or hard winds (Fig. 10–7). Plastic can be used for this type of wood, but it is easier to use real wood and break it into splinters. If you paint the wood with the same technique used to paint the plastic, you can mix wood and plastic as simulated wood in the same structure or fence.

Weathering Rocks and Cliffs

The Five-Step Weathering Technique will allow you to add effective superdetails to rocks and cliffs. Use precolored plaster and water-soluble paint with the staining techniques in Chapter 4 for rocks and cliffs placed several feet away from the viewer. For close-up scenes and dioramas, though, paint rock castings to compliment their textures and make them indistinguishable from real rocks using the technique Five-Step Weathering Technique. Look at your photographs of the area you are modeling to see if the real rocks and cliffs have moss growing on the north or well-shaded sides. About a quarter of all the

Fig. 10–2 Before: A typical HO-scale structure, converted from kits by *Model Railroading* magazine, before the weathering process.

Fig. 10–4 A wash of 19 parts water to 1 part Polly S black paint was applied to the structure to represent decades of rain-washed locomotive soot.

Fig. 10–3 Vintage Reproductions' dry transfers can be burnished onto the surface by rubbing the backing with a soft lead pencil.

Fig. 10–5 After: The weathered building shows decades of exposure to the elements.

Fig. 10–6 Rock faces near the foreground can be weathered to simulate the rough texture of real rocks.

rocks in any mountainous area have this effect. The Sage Green on Reference Card 16 in Chapter 5 is close to the color that is visible on most of the northern surfaces of rocks and cliffs in the Rocky Mountains and Sierras. Some additional gray or green can be added to simulate the colors of mosses in other areas, including the brighter green mosses near streams and lakes. The moss color should be applied as a paint, not a wash, using an airbrush to control the paint flow and give the spattered effect of real moss.

Weathering Signs

Any signs that you apply should show the effects of cracking or fading from wind or sun. These effects should be completed *before* using the Five-Step Weathering Technique. You can rub off portions of the sign with 600-grit emery paper or fine steel wool to simulate

Fig. 10–7 This HO-scale creosote company on the Sverna Park Model Railroad club layout shows years of neglect with broken boards, torn signs, and rain-washed soot and dirt.

the effects of wind and sun on the sign. Paper signs or advertisements on full-size structures can be duplicated with paper signs. Chooch offers full-color sheets of scale-size signs reproduced from advertisements from the 1930s to the present. You can also find suitable signs in magazines and even use cancelled postage stamps.

Paper signs should be treated with the following technique to reduce their thickness to something approximating scale-size paper. Place the cutout sign in a cup of water overnight. Remove the sign from the water and place it face down on a paper towel laid over a flat, hard surface. With your index finger, gently rub the back of the sign until little balls or threads of paper roll away. Continue rubbing until only the ink and a trace of paper remains. You may have to add more water during the process. Pick up the sign with tweezers and apply it to the wall or fence that has been coated with Bonding Agent (Reference Card 12 in Chapter 5). If necessary, dip your fingertip in water and press the paper sign firmly into the surface of the wall or fence. Allow the sign to dry for about three days, then weather it with 600-grit emery paper or fine steel wool. If fine hairs or fibers are still visible, spray the sign with a light coat of Testors "Dullcoate" and let it dry for a day. The paper can then be sanded again lightly with 600-grit emery paper to smooth the surface. The sign can now be weathered with the Five-Step Weathering Process.

Fig. 10–8 The weathering technique can be used for military dioramas, but with black to duplicate fire and smoke stains, as Russell Mueller did with Kurton's "Ruined Building" kit.

Battle Damage for Dioramas

The bomb-damaged diorama in Figure 10–8 shows how realistic the Five-Step Weathering Technique can be. Russell Mueller used cast-plaster walls from Kurton Products for the structures and balsa wood for the floors and loose beams. Kurton molds the loose brick and crumbling mortar effect directly into the material. The firm also offers products to simulate the piles of rubble. The Kurton Products kits are suitable for 1/48- through 1/35-scale dioramas. Some of the inexpensive Fundimensions/MPC/Airfix and the Lesney/Matchbox all-plastic diorama kits also have suitable battle-damaged walls for 1/87- through 1/76-scale dioramas. Individual bricks can be cut from balsa wood and added to the piles of rubble. Pile the rubble until you are satisfied with its shape, then form the piles into rigid units using Soaking Agent and Bonding Agent, as shown in Figures 5–3, 5–4, and 5–5 in Chapter 5.

Chapter 11

The Seasons and the Desert

One of the fundamental lessons of creating a credible model is to restrict that model to everyday scenes rather than dramatic ones. There is an extremely thin line between the unusual effects that nature produces and caricatures of nature. The beauty of an autumn scene, the stillness of a snow-covered station, or the drama of a desert are difficult to ignore as inspirations for any miniature scene. It certainly is possible to create a realistic diorama or model railroad with dramatic scenic effects, but it takes far more skill than modeling familiar scenes. The desert is included in this chapter because its character is as difficult to capture in miniature as an autumn or winter scene.

Autumn in Miniature

The brilliant rainbow of color that typifies autumn in the East and the golden yellow of aspens in the Rockies can be irresistible to modelers. The Buhl Planetarium's autumn diorama in the color section shows what can be accomplished with color. Dick Harley and Dave Hussey's aspen tree leaves are made with the paper punchings from check cancellations. The rainbow effect is easy to carry too far for a realistic scene; most of the colors you would *expect* to see are too bright to be realistic on a model. Buhl Planetarium's master modeler Charles Bowdish uses gray-white in the color mix to subdue the colors slightly. This makes them more pastel than those in a photograph of an eastern autumn. AMSI offers ground foam in autumn colors and Woodland Scenics produces "Foliage Material" in fall shades, so you do not necessarily have to create your own colors. If you find these brands

Fig. 11–1 Robert Schlachter used fine limbs from a real hedge for this 0-scale tree as it would appear in early spring.

to be too bright, a light wash of light gray Polly S paint can be sprayed over the trees to give the slightly hazy effect that is the most realistic for miniatures.

Winter Scenes

The snow-covered scenes of winter are well worth attempting, particularly for a diorama. If you don't want a complete winter diorama, you could duplicate winter's lingering snows near the tops of mountain passes. In some respects, a snow scene is even easier to create than a summer scene. The basic scenery shapes must still be constructed with the Hydrocal and paper-towels method, and any cliffs

Fig. 11–2 Betty and Laddy Dick used baking-soda "snow" in this HO-scale scene. The soda was sprinkled onto the rails, then "plowed" with a stick.

or other rock textures must be installed and painted. Roads should also be covered with dirt or simulated pavement. Other grass or dirt textures don't have to be installed, however, because the dirt and plants usually appear only on relatively gentle slopes, the same gentle slopes that would capture and hold snow. In place of the usual dirt, grass, and weed textures, you would substitute snow texture directly over the Hydrocal hills.

You may want to use molding plaster or plaster of paris to shape snowdrifts behind fences and on the roofs of cabins or other structures. Icicles can be made by stringing artist's gloss medium over a sheet of glass with a toothpick. Shape the icicles with several layers of the gloss medium and, after it dries, shave the icicles from the glass with a razor blade. Attach them to the eaves of buildings and rock cliffs to simulate frozen rivulets and springs with one of the thickened cyanoacrylates, such as Goldberg's "Super Jet" or Hot Stuff's "Super T."

Snow for Modelers

Every white powder known to man has been used by modelers to simulate snow. You can try your favorite, but be warned that nearly everything *except* common baking soda has some drawbacks. (Never use baking powder, which dissolves into a mudlike mess.) To apply baking-soda snow, spray the area with the Soaking Agent to moisten it (Reference Card 11 in Chapter 5). Pour on enough Bonding Agent to cover the area. The Bonding Agent will prevent the snow from scattering in unwanted areas. The baking soda can then be sprinkled over the area with a tea strainer (see Fig. 5–2). Tap the sides of the tea strainer with your finger to help control the flow of the baking soda.

Study some photos of winter scenes to be sure you're getting the snow into the right shapes and the right places. The roofs of moving railroad cars, for instance, seldom have visible snow, but it does accumulate on the pilots of locomotives. Standing freight cars accumulate as much snow as any nearby structures of course. The places where snow falls are fairly obvious, but remember to avoid placing snow in the areas where it would usually melt away. You can scrape the snow from the tops of railroad-track rails, but avoid getting it on any traveled portions of roads. To be safe, cut some newspaper masks to match the shape of the roads and hold them in place with map pins until you have completed the application of the snow. Simulate patches of ice and melted snow with dabs of artist's gloss medium.

The Desert

The desert in the United States is considered to be only the area around Phoenix, Arizona, where saguaro cactii grow (Figs. 1–10 and

Simulating Snow

Deep Drifts

Shape drifts with uncolored molding plaster or plaster of paris.

"Fresh" Snow

Shake baking soda (*not* baking powder) through a tea strainer to duplicate the effects of falling snow. For permanent snow, spray the area with a mixture of 2 parts water, 1 part artist's matte medium, and 4 drops dishwashing detergent per pint of water. Sift the baking soda into place while the area is still wet.

Icicles

Spread artist's gloss medium over a sheet of glass with a toothpick to form lumpy spikes. When dry, scrape the "icicles" from the glass with a single-edge razor blade and attach them to the eaves of buildings (or to waterfall areas) with Goldberg's "Super Jet" or Hot Stuff's "Super T" cement.

2–12). The cactus can be modeled with green pipe cleaners, but the ready-to-use "Cactus" from MLR Manufacturing are more realistic replicas of saguaro for 1/160 through 1/76 scales. More common to just about any desert scene are the relatively sparsely leafed mesquite and creosote bushes and clumps of yucca. These can be duplicated with fine-grind foam-textured lichen and macramé fiber as described in Chapter 6. Nearly all of these plants flower during the early spring, but the springlike effect is difficult to capture in miniature. Instead, re-create the desert the way it looks during the rest of the year.

The only portions of the desert that are flat are the bottoms of the dry lakes, and they, too, are difficult to simulate realistically. The

Fig. 11–3 Wally Suggs captured the isolation of the desert by positioning shrubs sparsely and by applying alternate shades of beige paint with an airbrush to simulate different sand colors.

seemingly flat portions of the desert are rolling hills and valleys with bare rock hills or mountains visible in the distance. Use rock castings extensively to capture this desert feeling. Of course real sand dominates any desert scene. Apply it the same way as dirt is used as a color and texture in Chapter 5.

Above all, the feeling of isolation must be captured, as Wally Suggs has with his N-scale modular scene (Fig. 11–3). The simulated road can be scraped into the sand with the edge of a coarse-textured ink eraser or a "Bright Boy" track-cleaning eraser. John built the Indian hogan from broken tree twigs and plaster of paris. He used several shades of beige and mixed traces of Boxcar Red, gray, yellow, and brown for the various sand tones. These color variations were mixed as washes or 1 part Polly S paint to 19 parts water to be sure the color changes were as subtle as possible. For illustrations of other desert scenes, see Figures 1–10 and 2–12.

Fig. 11–4 The dried roots of larger weeds, particularly the bushy "tumbleweed" variety, make realistic bare tree forms for use in winter scenes, as well as for dead and partially-dead trees in other seasons. Pull the weeds in late summer after a heavy rain so most of the tiny "hairs" remain, then trim and allow the root to dry for a month or more.

Sources of Supply

The best source for any scenery material is your nearest hobby dealer. Look in the telephone book's Yellow Pages under the heading "Hobby and Model Construction Supplies, Retail" for the names and addresses of the shops nearest you. If your local shop does not have exactly what you need, ask a salesperson to order it from the manufacturer. If you want to obtain the catalogs or other information from the manufacturer, always enclose a stamped, self-addressed envelope to ensure a reply. Most manufacturers charge for their catalogs, so ask for a current price. Some catalogs are only 25¢, but others are as high as $10.

AHM (see *Associated Hobby Manufacturers*)

A. I. M. Products
  P.O. Box 11860
  Winston-Salem, NC 27106

AMSI
  P.O. Box 3497
  San Rafael, CA 94902

Ambroid Company
  600 Water Street
  Taunton, MA 02780

Associated Hobby Manufacturers
  (Regal Way)
  200 Fifth Ave.
  Suite 717-19
  New York, NY 10010

Bachmann Industries, Inc.
  1400 East Erie Avenue
  Philadelphia, PA 19124

Campbell Scale Models, Inc.
  P.O. Box 121
  Tustin, CA 92680

Celluclay (see Ambroid)

Chama Timber Company
Box 749
Chama, NM 87520

CHEMCO
P.O. Box 883
San Leandro, CA 94577

Chooch Enterprises
Box 217
Redmond, WA 98052

Color-Rite Scenery Products
2041 Winnetka North
Minneapolis, MN 55247

Creative Screen Process
555 East Airline Way
Gardena, CA 90248

Detail Associates
Box 197
Santa Maria, CA 93456

Envirotex (Enviromental
Technology, Inc.)
South Bay Depot Road
Fields Landing, CA 95537

Faller (see Walthers)

Floquil-Polly S Corporation
Route 30 North
Amsterdam, NY 12010

Fundimensions/MPC/Airfix
26750 23-Mile Road
Mount Clemens, MI 48045

Glidden (*see the Yellow Pages under "Paint, Retail"*)

Gold Seal Creations, Inc.
1588 Loconder Crescent
Mississauga, Ontario, L5C
1T1, Canada

HO West! (*see Walthers*)

Highball Products
4527 Reading Road
Cincinnati, OH 45243

Hydrocal (*see U.S. Gypsum
Corporation*)

I.S.L.E. Laboratories
P.O. Box 636
Sylvania, OH 43560

JMC International
1025 Industrial Drive
Bensenville, IL 60106

John's Lab
4915 Dean Street
Woodstock, IL 60098

Johnson's All-Scale Trees
RD No. 1
Milton, PA 17847

Kibri (*see Walthers or JMC
International*)

Krasel Industries, Inc.
1821 East Newport Circle
Santa Ana, CA 92705

Kurton Products
P.O. Box 7446
Colorado Springs, CO 80933

LaBelle Industries
P.O. Box 328
Bensenville, IL 60106

Lesney/Matchbox
  Irwin Toy Ltd.
  165 N. Queen St.
  Etobicoke, Ontario, Canada
  M9C 1A7

Life-Like Products, Inc.
  1600 Union Avenue
  Baltimore, MD 21211

Merten (*see JMC International or Walthers*)

Micro Scale (*see Krase Industries*)

MLR Manufacturing Company
  P.O. Box 1051
  Carlisle, PA 92008

Modern Mache (*see Gold Seal Creations, Inc.*)

Mountains-in-Minutes (*see I.S.L.E. Laboratories*)

Noch (*see JMC International or Walthers*)

Paul's Model Railroad Shop
  121 Lincolnway West
  New Oxford, PA 17350

Polly S (*see Floquil-Polly S Corporation*)

Preiser (*see Walthers or JMC International*)

Ribbons Stiehl (*see Walthers*)

Scenic Craft, Inc.
  Box 862
  Edmond, OK 73034

Sommerfeldt (*see Paul's Model Railroad Shop*)

U.S. Gypsum Corporation (for the name of your nearest Hydrocal dealer, call 800-621-9532)

Vintage Reproductions
  Box 7098
  Colorado Springs, CO 80933

Vollmer (*see Walthers or JMC International*)

Wm K. Walthers, Inc.
  5601 West Florist Avenue
  Milwaukee, WI 53218

Woodland Scenics
  P.O. Box 98
  Linn Creek, MO 65052

Yankee Junction
  P.O. Box 211
  Glen, NH 03838

Index

Boldface page numbers refer to illustrations